MARRIAGE
OF
HINDU WIDOWS

MARRIAGE OF HINDU WIDOWS

ISHVARCHANDRA VIDYASAGAR

GYAN

Published by

GYAN

Gyan Publishing House
5, Ansari Road
Daryaganj, New Delhi-110002
Phone: 011-47034999, 9811692060
E-mail: books@gyanbooks.com

Distribution Network
gyanbooks.com
India, USA, Canada, UK, Australia

ISBN: 978-93-7169-331-8 (PB)

First Published, 1864

2nd Impression 2025

Printed at: Gyan Press, Delhi.

MARRIAGE OF HINDU WIDOWS
Author: ISHVARCHANDRA VIDYASAGAR

MARRIAGE

OF

HINDU WIDOWS

BY

ISWARACHANDRA VIDYASAGARA.

SECOND EDITION.

CALCUTTA:

THE SANSKRIT PRESS.

1864.

PREFACE.

In January 1855, I published a small pamphlet in Bengali on the marriage of Hindu Widows, with the view to prove that it was sanctioned by the Sastras. To this pamphlet, replies were given by many of my countrymen. Instead of a rejoinder to each of them, I published, in October last, a second pamphlet in the same language, in which I noticed the material objections of all my Replicants.

The subject under discussion being of a nature which concerned my countrymen only, I had, as stated, published my pamphlets in Bengali and had no intention to issue an English version of them. But I was obliged to change my mind, because I found that since the publication of my pamphlets. several parties attempted to misrepresent things to the English public in Reviews and Journals. To these, I was pressed by my friends to reply, but as it appeared to me that my pamphlets met all the objections that might be urged against the legality of the marriage of Hindu widows, I thought it best to publish an English version of them, which I now lay respectfully before the English Public.

Other parties have again gone so far as to assert

that in my treatment of the subject, I have been influenced more by compassion towards the unfortunate widows of my country than by a firm belief in their remarriage being consonant to the Sastras. They have also said that to prove such consonance is an impossibility. It is true that I do feel compassion for our miserable widows, but at the same time I may be permitted to state, that I did not take up my pen before I was fully convinced that the Sastras explicitly sanction their remarriage. This conviction I have come to, after a diligent, dispassionate and careful examination of the subject and I can now safely affirm, that in the whole range of our original Smritis there is not one single Text which can establish any thing to the contrary.

The translation is neither entire nor literal. The original, having been intended for the mass of the native population, was written in a manner which would best suit their understandings. But as the English version has been prepared for a different class of Readers, I have been obliged to omit several passages in the second pamphlet to avoid repetition and occasionally to add or alter other passages, to make the translation suitable to them. For the same reason, several Chapters, which treat of comparatively unimportant points and may not be interesting to the English Public, have been altogether omitted.

MARRIAGE OF HINDU WIDOWS.

Many Hindus are now thoroughly convinced of the pernicious consequences arising from the practice of prohibiting the Marriage of widows. Many are already prepared to give their widowed daughters, sisters and other relations in Marriage, and those, who dare not go so far, acknowledge it to be most desirable that this should be done.

Whether the marriage of widows is consonant to our Sastras, is a question which, a short while ago, was discussed by some of the principal Pundits of our country. But, unfortunately, our modern Pundits, carried away, in the heat of controversy, by a passion for victory, become so eager to maintain their respective dogmas that they entirely lose sight ot the subject they are investigating; and hence there is no hope of arriving at the truth of any question by convening an assembly of Pundits and setting them to debate on it. At the discussion above alluded to, each party considered itself victorious and its antagonist foiled. It is easy, therefore, to conceive how the question was decided. In fact, nothing was settled as to the point at issue. One great object, however, has been gained, and that is that most people, since that period, have been extremely anxious to ascertain the truth of this matter. Perceiving this eagerness I have been led to enquire into the subject ; and, in order to lay before the public at large the result of my enquiries, I publish this treatise in the vernacular language of the country : so that after an impartial examination the Hindu public may judge whether the marriage of widows ought to be practised or not.

In entering upon this enquiry we should, first of all, consider that, since the marriage of widows is a custom which has not prevailed among Hindus for many ages, in seeking to give our widows in marriage we propose an innovation and are bound to shew that the custom is a proper one ; for if it be otherwise, no man, having any regard for religion, would consent to its introduction. It is, therefore, highly necessary to establish first the propriety of this custom. But how is this to be done ? By reasoning alone ? No. For it will not be admitted by our countrymen that *mere* reasoning is applicable to such subjects. The custom must have the sanction of the Sastras ; for in matters like this, the Sastras are the paramount authority among Hindus, and such acts only as are conformable to them are deemed proper. It must, therefore, first be settled, whether the marriage of widows is a custom consonant or opposed to the Sastras.

At the very outset of the enquiry as to whether the marriage of widows is consonant or opposed to our Sastras, we find it necessary to decide what are those

Sastras, the sanction or prohibition of which will determine the propriety or impropriety of the practice. Certainly, Vyakarana (Grammar), Kavya (Poetry), Alankara (Rhetoric), Darsana (Philosophy) and the like are not Sastras of this kind. It is only the works known as Dharma Sastras, that is to say, the works comprising the whole body of ceremonial and religious observances, moral duties, and municipal law, that are every where regarded as the Sastras to be referred to in deciding such questions.

In the first chapter of the Yajnavalkya-Sanhita there is an enumeration of what are called the Dharma Sastras; namely,

मन्वत्रिविष्णुहारीतयाज्ञवल्क्योशनोऽङ्गिराः ।
यमापस्तम्बसंवर्ताः कात्यायनबृहस्पती ॥
पराशरव्यासशङ्खलिखिता दक्षगोतमौ ।
शातातपो वशिष्ठश्च धर्मशास्त्रप्रयोजकाः ॥

"Manu, Atri, Vishnu, Harita, Yajnavalkya, Usana, Angira, Yama, Apastamba, Saubarta, Katyayana, Vrihaspati, Parasara, Vyasa, Saukha, Likhita, Daksha, Gotama, Satatapa, and Vasishtha are the authors of the Dharma Sastras."

The Sastras promulgated by these Rishis (Sages) are the Dharma Sastras.* The people of India (Hindus) observe those Dharmas (duties) which are enjoined in these Sastras; and acts are considered proper or impro-

* Besides these, the Sastras promulgated by Narada, Baudhayana and fourteen other *Rishis* are also reckoned as Dharma Sastras.

per according as they are consonant or opposed to these Dharma Sastras. Hence the marriage of widows will be countenanced, if conformable, and repudiated, if repugnant, to the Dharma Sastras.

Now it is to be considered whether all the Dharmas inculcated in all the Dharma Sastras are to be observed in all the Yugas (Ages). There is a solution of this question in the first chapter of the Dharma Sastra of Manu :

अन्ये कृतयुगे धर्मास्त्रेतायां द्वापरेऽपरे ।
अन्ये कलियुगे नृणां युगह्रासानुरूपतः ॥

"Human power decreasing according to the Yugas, the "Dharmas of the Satya Yuga are one thing, those of the "Treta another ; the Dharmas of the Dwapara are one "thing, those of the Kali another."

That is to say, the Dharmas, which the people of prior Yugas practised cannot now be observed by the people of the Kali Yuga, because human power decreases in every successive Yuga. Men of the Treta Yuga had not the power of observing the Dharmas of the Satya Yuga, those of the Dwapara could not observe the Dharmas of either the Satya or Treta Yuga, and those of the Kali Yuga lack strength to follow the Dharmas of the Satya, Treta or Dwapara Yuga.

It clearly appears, then, that the people of the Kali Yuga are unable to practise the Dharmas of the past Yugas ; and the question arises what are those Dharmas which the people of the Kali Yuga are to observe. In the Dharma Sastra of Manu it is merely stated that there are different Dharmas for the different Yugas ; but the Dharmas peculiar to the different Yugas have not been specified. Neither in the Dharma Sastras of Atri, Vishnu, Harita and others mention is made of these different Dharmas. Certain Dharmas are indeed inculcated in these Dharma Sastras ; but it is difficult to determine the Dharmas which, owing to the decrease of human power in successive Yugas, are appropriate to each Yuga. It is in the Parásara Sanhita only that there is an assignment of the Dharmas peculiar to the different Yugas. Thus it is mentioned in the first chapter of the Parasara Sanhita :

कृते तु मानवा धर्मास्त्रेतायां गौतमाः स्मृताः ।
द्वापरे शाङ्खलिखिताः कलौ पाराशराः स्मृताः ॥

"The Dharmas enjoined by Manu are assigned to the Satya Yuga ; those by Gotama to the Treta ; those by Sankha and Likhita to the Dwapara ; and those by Parasara, to the kali Yuga."

That is, the people of the Satya, Treta and Dwapara practised the Dharmas prescribed by Manu, Gotama, and Sankha and Likhita respectively ; and the people of the Kali Yuga are to observe the Dharmas prescribed by Parasara.* It is clear, therefore, that as Parasara has

* It may be asked if the Dharma Sastras promulgated by Manu alone were to be followed in the Satya Yuga, that of Gotama alone in the Treta, that of Sankha and Likhita alone in the Dwapara and that of

prescribed the Dharmas of the Kali Yuga, the people of the Kali Yuga ought to follow the Dharmas prescribed by him.

On observing how the Parasara Sanhita opens, there will not remain the shadow of a doubt that its sole object is to promulgate the Dharmas of the Kali Yuga.

अथातो हिमशैलाग्रे देवदारुवनालये ।
व्यासमेकाग्रमासीनमपृच्छन्नृषयः पुरा ॥
मानुषाणां हितं धर्म्मं वर्त्तमाने कलौ युगे ।
शौचाचारं यथावच्च वद सत्यवतीसुत ॥
तच्छ्रुत्वा ऋषिवाक्यन्तु सशिष्योऽग्न्यर्कसन्निभः ।
प्रत्युवाच महातेजाः श्रुतिस्मृतिविशारदः ॥
न चाहं सर्व्वतत्त्वज्ञः कथं धर्मं वदाम्यहम् ।
अस्मत्पितैव प्रष्टव्य इति व्यासः सुतोऽवदत् ॥
ततस्ते ऋषयः सर्व्वे धर्मतत्त्वार्थकाङ्क्षिणः ।
ऋषिं व्यासं पुरस्कृत्य गता बदरिकाश्रमम् ॥
नानावृक्षसमाकीर्णं फलपुष्पोपशोभितम् ।
नदीप्रस्रवणाकीर्णं पुण्यतीर्थैरलङ्कृतम् ॥
मृगपक्षिनिनादाढ्यं देवतायतनावृतम् ।
यक्षगन्धर्व्वसिद्धैश्च नृत्यगीतसमाकुलम् ॥
तस्मिन्नृषिसभामध्ये शक्तिपुत्रं पराशरम् ।

Parasara alone in the Kali Yuga, when all the Dharma Sastras composed by the other sages to be observed. But this question admits of an easy solution. The Dharma Sastras of Manu, of Gotama, of Sankha and Likhita and of Parasara are peculiar to the Satya, Treta, Dwapara and Kali respectively and such parts of the other Dharma Sastras as are not at variances with those prominent Sastras are to be followed in those Yugas.

सुखासीनं महात्मानं मुनिमुख्यगणावृतम् ॥
कृताञ्जलिपुटो भूत्वा व्यासस्तु ऋषिभिः सह ।
प्रदक्षिणाभिवादैश्च स्तुतिभिः समपूजयत् ॥
अथ सन्तुष्टमनसा पराशरमहामुनिः ।
आह सुस्वागतं ब्रूहीत्यासीनो मुनिपुङ्गवः ॥
व्यासः सुस्वागतं ये च ऋषयश्च समन्ततः ।
कुशलं कुशलेत्युक्त्वा व्यासः पृच्छत्ततःपरम् ॥
यदि जानासि मे भक्तिं स्नेहाद्वा भक्तवत्सल ।
धर्मं कथय मे तात अनुग्राह्यो ह्यहं तव ॥
श्रुता मे मानवा धर्मा वाशिष्ठाः काश्यपास्तथा ।
गार्गेया गौतमाश्चैव तथा चौशनसाः श्रुताः ॥
अत्रेर्विष्णोश्च संवर्त्ताः दाक्षा आङ्गिरसास्तथा ।
शातातपाश्च हारीता याज्ञवल्क्यकृताश्च ये ॥
कात्यायनकृताश्चैव प्राचेतसकृताश्च ये ।
आपस्तम्बकृता धर्माः शङ्खस्य लिखितस्य च ॥
श्रुता ह्येते भवत्प्रोक्ताः श्रुत्यर्थास्ते न विस्मृताः ।
अस्मिन् मन्वन्तरे धर्माः कृतत्रेतादिके युगे ॥
सर्वे धर्माः कृते जाताः सर्वे नष्टाः कलौ युगे ।
चातुर्वर्ण्यसमाचारं किञ्चित् साधारणं वद ॥
व्यासवाक्यावसाने तु मुनिमुख्यः पराशरः ।
धर्मस्य निर्णयं प्राह सूक्ष्मं स्थूलञ्च विस्तरात् ॥

" In times of yore some Rishis thus addressed Vyasadeva : Declare to us, oh son of Satyavati ! what are the Dharmas and Acharas (practices) beneficial to men in the Kali Yuga. Vyasadeva, on hearing these words of the Rishis, said as I know not the truth of all things how shall I declare the Dharmas. My father should be consulted on the subject. Then the Rishis, accompanying Vyasadeva, arrived at the retreat of Parasara. Vyasadeva and the Rishis, with joined palms, circumambulated, saluted and glorified Parasara. The great Rishi Parasara having welcomed them with a joyous heart and made enquiries, they informed him of their own welfare. After which Vyasadeva said, Oh Sire! I have heard from you, the Dharmas peculiar to the Satya, Treta and Dwapara as prescribed by Manu and others; what I have heard, I have not forgotten. All the Dharmas originated in the Satya Yuga, all of them have expired in the Kali Yuga. Declare, therefore, some of the common Dharmas of the four varnas (castes). On the conclusion of Vyasa's speech, the great Rishi Parasara began to declare the Dharmas in detail."

At the commencement of the 2nd chapter also of the Parasara Sanhita, there plainly appears a resolution to speak the Dharmas peculiar to the Kali Yuga. Thus :—

अतःपरं गृहस्थस्य धर्म्माचारं कलौ युगे।
धर्म्मं साधारणं शक्यं चातुर्वर्ण्याश्रमागतम्॥
संप्रवक्ष्याम्यहं पूर्व्वं पराशरवचो यथा॥

"Now, I shall declare the Dharmas and Acharas to be practised by a Grihastha (Householder) in the Kali Yuga. I shall first declare the practicable Dharmas common to the four varnas (castes) and Asramas (orders) as taught by Parasara."

After all this, it can neither be denied nor questioned that the Parasara Sanhita is the Dharma Sastra of the Kali Yuga.

Now, it should be enquired, what Dharmas have been enjoined in the Parasara Sanhita for widows. We find in the 4th chapter of this work the following passage :—

> नष्टे मृते प्रव्रजिते क्लीबे च पतिते पतौ ।
> पञ्चस्वापत्सु नारीणां पतिरन्यो विधीयते ॥
> मृते भर्त्तरि या नारी ब्रह्मचर्य्ये व्यवस्थिता ।
> सा मृता लभते स्वर्गं यथा ते ब्रह्मचारिणः ॥
> तिस्रः कोट्योऽर्द्धकोटी च यानि लोमानि मानवे ।
> तावत् कालं वसेत् स्वर्गं भर्त्तारं यानुगच्छति ॥

" On receiving no tidings of a husband, on his demise, on his turning an ascetic, on his being found impotent or on his degradation—under any one of these five calamities, it is canonical for women to take another husband. That woman, who on the decease of her husband observes the Brahmacharya (leads the life of austerities and privations), attains heaven after death. She, who burns herself with her deceased husband, resides in heaven for as many Kalas or thousands of years as there are hairs on the human body or thirty-five millions."

Thus it appears that Parasara prescribes three rules for the conduct of a widow ; marriage, the observance of the Brahmacharya and burning with the deceased husband. Among these, the custom of concremation has been abolished by order of the ruling authorities ; only two ways, therefore, have now been left for the widows ; they have the option of marrying or of observing the Brahmacharya. But in the Kali Yuga, it has become extremely difficult for widows to pass their lives in the observance of the Brahmacharya and it is for this reason, that the Philanthropic Parasara has, in the first instance, prescribed marriage. Be that as it may, what I wish to be clearly understood is this—that as Parasara plainly prescribes marriage as one of the duties of women in the Kali Yuga under any one of the five above enumerated calamities, the marriage of widows in the Kali Yuga is consonant to the Sastras.

It being settled that the marriage of widows in the Kali Yuga is consonant to the Sastras, we should now consider whether the son born of a widow on her re-marriage, should be called a Paunarbhava.* There is a solution of this question in the Parasara Sanhita itself. Twelve different sorts of sons were sanctioned by the Sastras in the former Yugas, but Parasara has reduced their number to three for the Kali Yuga. Thus :

औरसः क्षेत्रजश्चैव दत्तः कृत्रिमकः सुतः ।

"The Aurasa (son of the body or son by birth), the Dattaka (son adopted), and the Kritrima (son made)."†

* A son born of a woman married a second time. In the prior Yugas the Paunarbha was considered as an inferior sort of son.

† In the Text there appears an enumeration of four different sorts of sons, but *Nanda Pandita* in his *Dattaka Mimansa*, has, by his interpretation of this passage, established that there are only three different sorts of sons in the Kali Yuga, the son of the body, the son adopted and the son made. I have followed his interpretation.

Parasara, then, ordains three different sorts of sons in the Kali Yuga, the son by birth, the son adopted, and the son made; and makes no mention of the Paunarbhava. But as he has prescribed the marriage of widows he has, in effect, legalized the son born of a widow in lawful wedlock.

Now, the question to be decided is, whether this son should be called Aurasa (son of the body), Dattaka (son adopted), or Kritrima (son made). He can neither be called Dattaka nor Kritrima, for the son of another man, adopted agreeably to the injuctions of the Sastras is called Dattaka or Kritrima according to the difference of the ritual observed during the adoption. But since the son begotten by a man himself on the widow to whom he is married, is not another's son, he can be designated by neither of those appellations. The definitions of Dattaka (son adopted) and Kritrima (son made) as given in the Sastras, cannot be applied to the son begotten by a man himself on the widow married to him, but he falls under the description of the Aurasa (son by birth). Thus:—

माता पिता वा दद्यातां यमद्भिः पुत्रमापदि ।
सदृशं प्रीतिसंयुक्तं स ज्ञेयो दत्त्रिमः सुतः ॥

" The son given, according to the injunctions of the Sastras, by either of his parents, with a contented mind, to a person of the same caste, who has no male issuc, is the Dattaka (son adopted) of the donce."

सदृशन्तु प्रकुर्य्याद्यं गुणदोषविचक्षणम् ।
पुत्रं पुत्रगुणैर्युक्तं स विज्ञेयश्च कृत्रिमः ॥

" He, who is endowed with filial virtues and well acquainted with merits and demerits, when affiliated by a person of the same class, is called Kritrima (son made)."

स्वे क्षेत्रे संस्कृतायान्तु स्वयमुत्पादयेद्धि यम्।
तमौरसं विजानीयात् पुत्रं प्रथमकल्पितम्॥*

" Whom a man himself has begotten on a woman of the same class, to whom he is married, know him to be the Aurasa (son of the body) and the first in rank."

The indicia of an Aurasa (son by birth) as above set forth, apply therefore, with full force to the son begotten by a man himself on a widow of the same class to whom he is wedded.

Since the Parasara Sanhita prescribes the marriage of widows and out of twelve legalizes only three sorts of sons in the Kali Yuga ; since the indicia of the Dattaka (son adopted), and of the Kritrima (son made), do not apply to the son born of a widow in lawful wedlock, while those of the Aurasa (son by birth), apply to him with full force, we are authorized to recognize him as the Aurasa or the son of the body. It can by no means be established that Parasara intended to reckon the son of a wedded widow in the Kali Yuga as a Paunarbhava by which name such a son was designated in the former Yugas ; and had it been necessary to give him the same designation in the Kali Yuga, Parasara would certainly have included the Paunarbhava in his enumeration of the different

* Manu Ch. IX.

sorts af sons in the Kali Yuga. But far from this. The term Paunarbhava is not to be found in the Parasara Sanhita. There can be no doubt, therefore, that in the Kali Yuga, the son begotten by a person himself on the widow to whom he is wedded, instead of being called Paunarbhava, will be reckoned as the Aurasa.

It being settled by the arguments above cited, that the marriage of widows in the Kali Yuga is consonant to the Sastras, we should, now, enquire whether in any Sastras, other than the Parasara Sanhita, there is a prohibition of this marriage in the Kali Yuga. For it is argued by many that the marriage of widows was in vogue in the former Yugas, but has been forbidden in the Kali Yuga. It should be remembered, however, that in the Parasara Sanhita the Dharmas, appropriated to the Kali Yuga only, have been assigned and among those Dharmas the marriage of widows has been prescribed in the clearest manner. It can, therefore, never be maintained that widows have been forbidden to marry in the Kali Yuga. Under what authority this prohibitory dogma is upheld, is a secret known only to the prohibitionists.

Some people consider the texts of the Vrihannaradiya and Aditya Puranas, quoted by the Smartta Bhattacharya Raghunandana in his article on marriage, as prohibitory of the marriage of widows in the Kali Yuga. Those texts are, therefore, cited here with an explanation of their meaning and purport.

Vrihannaradiya Purana.

समुद्रयात्रास्वीकारः कमण्डलुविधारणम् ।
द्विजानामसवर्णासु कन्यासूपयमस्तथा ॥
देवरेण सुतोत्पत्तिर्मधुपर्के पशोर्वधः ।
मांसादनं तथा श्राद्धे वानप्रस्थाश्रमस्तथा ॥
दत्तायाश्चैव कन्यायाः पुनर्दानं परस्य च ।
दीर्घकालं ब्रह्मचर्यं नरमेधाश्वमेधकौ ॥
महाप्रस्थानगमनं गोमेधश्च तथा मखम् ।
इमान् धर्मान् कलियुगे वर्ज्यानाहुर्मनीषिणः ॥

"Sea voyage; turning an ascetic; the marriage of twice-born men with damsels not of the same class; procreation on a brother's wife or widow; the slaughter of cattle in the entertainment of a guest; the repast on flesh-meat at funeral obsequies; the entrance into the order of a Vanaprastha (hermit); the giving away of a damsel, a second time, to a bridegroom, after she has been given to another; Brahmacharya continued for a long time; the sacrifice of a man, horse, or bull; walking on a pilgrimage till the Pilgrim die, are the Dharmas the observance of which has been forbidden by the Munis (sages) in the Kali Yuga."

Nowhere in these texts can any passage be found forbidding the marriage of widows. Those, who try to establish this forbiddance on the strength of the prohibition of "the giving away of a damsel, a second time, to a bridegroom, after she has been given to another", have misunderstood the real purport of this passage. In former times, there prevailed a custom of marrying a damsel, who has been betrothed to a suitor, to another bridegroom when found to be endued with superior qualities. Thus :

सकृत् प्रदीयते कन्या हरंस्तां चौरदण्डभाक्।
दत्तामपि हरेत् पूर्व्वात् श्रेयांश्चेद्वर आव्रजेत्॥*

"A damsel can be given away but once; and he, who takes her back after having given away, incurs the penalty of theft : but even a damsel given may be taken back from the prior bridegroom, if a worthier suitor offer himself."

The Vrihannaradiya Purana alludes only to the prohibition of the custom, prevailing in the former Yugas and sanctioned by the Sastras, of marrying a girl betrothed to one person, to a worthier suitor. It is absurd, therefore, to construe the prohibition into a forbiddance of the marriage of widows in the Kali Yuga. Nor is it reasonable to understand this text of the Vrihannaradiya Purana, by a forced construction, as prohibitory of such marriage, while the plainest and the most direct injunction for it is to be found in the Parasara Sanhita.

Aditya Purana.

दीर्घकालं ब्रह्मचर्य्यं धारणञ्च कमण्डलोः।
देवरेण सुतोत्पत्तिर्दत्ता कन्या प्रदीयते॥
कन्यानामसवर्णानां विवाहश्च द्विजातिभिः।
आततायिद्विजाग्र्याणां धर्म्मयुद्धेन हिंसनम्॥
वानप्रस्थाश्रमस्यापि प्रवेशो विधिदेशितः।
वृत्तस्वाध्यायसापेक्षमघसङ्कोचनं तथा॥

* Yajnavalkya Sanhita. Ch. I.

प्रायश्चित्तविधानञ्च विप्राणां मरणान्तिकम् ।
संसर्गदोषः पापेषु मधुपर्के पशोर्वधः ॥
दत्तौरसेतरेषान्तु पुत्रत्वेन परिग्रहः ।
शूद्रेषु दासगोपालकुलमित्रार्द्धसीरिणाम् ॥
भोज्यान्नता गृहस्थस्य तीर्थसेवातिदूरतः ।
ब्राह्मणादिषु शूद्रस्य पक्वतादिक्रियापि च ।
भृग्वग्निपतनञ्चैव वृद्धादिमरणं तथा ॥
एतानि लोकगुप्त्यर्थं कलेरादौ महात्मभिः ।
निवर्त्तितानि कर्म्माणि व्यवस्थापूर्वकं बुधैः ॥

"Long continued Brahmacharya ; turning an ascetic ; procreation on a brother's wife or widow ; the gift of a girl already given ; the marriage of the twice-born men with damsels not of the same class ; the killing of Brahmanas, intent upon destruction, in a fair combat ; entrance into the order of a Vanaprastha (hermit) ; the diminution of the period of Asaucha (impurity) in proportion to the purity of character and the extent of erudition in the Vedas ; the rule of expiation for Brahmanas extending to death ; the sin of holding intercourse with sinners ; the slaughter of cattle in the entertainment of a guest ; the filiation of sons other than the Dattaka (son adopted) and the Aurasa (son by birth) ; the eating of edibles by a Grihastha (Householder) of the twice-born class, offered to him by a Dasa, Gopala, Kulamitra and Ardhasiri of the Sudra caste ; the undertaking of a distant pilgrimage ; the cooking of a Brahmana's meat by a Sudra ; falling from a precipice ; entrance into fire ; the self dissolution of old and other men —these have been legally abrogated, in the beginning of the

Kali Yuga, by the wise and magnanimous, for the protection of men."

Nowhere also in these texts can any passage be found prohibiting the marriage of widows. That the interdict of the "gift of a girl already given," cannot be construed into such a prohibition, has already been shewn in examining a similar interdictory passage in the Vrihannaradiya Purana.

Some people say, that the prohibition of the filiation of sons other than the Aurasa (son by birth) and the Dattaka (son adopted) in the Aditya Purana leads to the forbiddance of the marriage of widows. They argue in the following manner,— In the former Yugas, the sons of widows, born in wedlock, were called Paunarbhavas; now, as there is a prohibition to filiate any other sons in the Kali Yuga except the Aurasa (son by birth) and the Dattacka (son adopted), this prohibition extends to the filiation of the Paunarbhava: the object of marriage is to have male issue; but if the filiation of the Paunarbhava begotten on a wedded widow be interdicted, the marriage of widows is necessarily interdicted.—This objection appears, at first sight, rather strong and, in the absence of Parasara Sanhita, would have succeeded in establishing the prohibition of the marriage of widows. But they, who raise this objection, have not, I believe, seen the Parasara Sanhita. It is true, indeed, that in the former Yugas, the son of a wedded widow was called Paunarbhava; but from what I have argued above in respect of the application of the term Paunarbhava to the son of a wedded widow in the Kali Yuga, it has been already decided that the distinction between a Paunarbhava and an Aurasa has been done away with. If then the son, born of a widow in lawful wedlock, instead of being called a Paunarbhava, be reckoned as Aurasa in the Kali Yuga, how can the prohibition, in the Kali Yuga, of the filiation of sons other than the Aurasa and Dattaka lead to the interdiction of the marriage of widows in the Kali Yuga?

It will now appear from the manner, in which I have expounded the spirit of the above quoted Texts of the Vrihannaradiya and Aditiya Puranas, that they do not prohibit the marriage of widows in the Kali Yuga. But if the prohibitionists, not satisfied with the explanation, contend against the consonancy of this marriage to the Sastras, by citing the above Texts as prohibitory of the marriage of widows, we have then to consider the following question: The marriage of widows is enforced in the Parasara Sanhita, but interdicted in the Vrihannaradiya and Aditya Puranas; which of them is the stronger authority? That is, whether, according to the injunction of Parasara, the marriage of widows is to be considered legal, or, according to the interdiction of the Vrihannaradiya and Aditya Puranas, it is to be held illegal.

To settle this point, we should enquire what decision the authors of our Sastras have come to in judging of the cogency of two classes of authorities, when they differ from each other. The auspicious Vedavyasa has, in his own institutes, settled this point, Thus:—

श्रुतिस्मृतिपुराणानां विरोधो यत्र दृश्यते।
तत्र श्रौतं प्रमाणन्तु तयोर्द्वैधे स्मृतिर्वरा॥

"Where variance is observed between the Veda, the Smriti and the Purana, there the Veda is the supreme authority: when the Smriti and the Purana contradict each other, the Smriti is the superior authority."

That is, when the Veda inculcate one thing, the Smriti another and the Purana a third, what is then to be done? which Sastra is to be followed? Men ought to regard all the three as Sastras, and if they follow only one of them, they disregard the other two; and by a disrespect of the Sastras they incur sin. The auspicious Vedavyasa, therefore, has settled the point, by declaring that when the Veda, the Smriti and the Purana are at variance with each other, then we should, instead of following the injunctions of the latter two, act up to those of the former; and in the event of a contradiction between the Smriti and the Purana, we should, instead of following the ordinances of the latter, act up to those of the former.

Mark now, in the first place, that from the above exposition of the Vrihannaradiya and Aditya Puranas, they do, by no means, appear to prohibit the marriage of widows: secondly, if by any forced construction, they can be made to imply such a prohibition, then there arises a palpable contradiction between the Vrihanaradiya and Aditya Puranas, and the Parasara Sanhita. The Parasara Sanhita prescribes, and the Vrihannaradiya and

Aditya Puranas interdict, the marriage of widows in the Kali Yuga. The Parasara Sanhita is one of the Smritis, while the Vrihannaradiya and Aditya Puranas are Puranas. The author of the Puranas himself ordains, that when the Smriti and the Purana differ from each other, the former is to be followed in preference to the latter. Hence, even if the Texts of the Vrihannaradiya and Aditya Puranas were made to imply a prohibition of the marriage of widows in the Kali Yuga, we should, in spite of it, follow the positive injunction for the marriage of widows in the Parasara Sanhita.

It can now be safely concluded that the consonancy of the marriage of widows to our Sastras has been indisputably settled. A fresh objection, however, may now arise that though the marriage of widows be sanctioned by our Sastras, yet being opposed to approved custom, it should not be practised. To answer this objection, it should be enquired in what case is approved custom to be followed as an authority. The Auspicious Vasishtha has settled this point in his institutes. Thus:

लोके प्रेत्य वा विहितो धर्मः ।
तदलाभे शिष्टाचारः प्रमाणम् ॥

"Whether in matters connected with this or the next world, in both cases, the Dharmas inculcated by the Sastras are to be observed: where there is an omission in the Sastras, *there* approved custom is the authority."

That is, men should observe those duties which have been inculcated by the Sastras; and in cases where the

Sastras prescribe no rule or make no prohibition, but at the same time a practice, followed by a succession of virtuous ancestors, prevails, then such practice is to be deemed equal in authority to an ordinance of the Sastras. Now, as there is in the Parasara Sanhita a plain injunction for the marriage of widows in the Kali Yuga, it is neither reasonable nor consonant to the Sastras to consider it an illicit act, merely because it is opposed to approved usage; for it is ordained by Vasishtha that approved custom is to be followed only in cases where there is an omission in the Sastras. It is, therefore, indisputably proved that the marriage of widows, in the Kali Yuga, is, in all respects, a proper act.

An adequate idea of the intolerable hardships of early widowhood can be formed by those only whose daughters, sisters, daughters-in-law and other female relatives have been deprived of their husbands during their infancy. How many hundreds of widows, unable to observe the austerities of a Brahmacharya life, betake themselves to prostitution and fœticide and thus bring disgrace upon the families of their fathers, mothers and husbands. If the marriage of widows be allowed, it will remove the insupportable torments of life-long widowhood, diminish the crimes of prostitution and fœticide and secure all families from disgrace and infamy. As long as this salutary practice will be deferred, so long will the crimes of prostitution, adultery, incest and fœticide flow on in an ever increasing current—so long will family stains be multiplied—so long will a widow's agony blaze on in fiercer flames.

In conclusion, I humbly beseech the public to attend to these circumstances, and after having duly weighed all that have been said respecting the consonancy of the marriage of widows to the Sastras, to decide whether the marriage of widows should or should not prevail ?

MARRIAGE OF HINDU WIDOWS.

THE REJOINDER.

When the question of introducing the practice of the Marriage of Widows was first laid before the Community, I had strong apprehensions that it would be regarded with contempt; that the very title and purport of the work, which I published on the subject, would be a drawback to its attentive perusal and that consequently my labour would be thrown away. But I was agreeably disappointed to find the public so eager to obtain the work, that, shortly after its publication, and in less than a week, its first impression, consisting of two thousand copies, was entirely exhausted. I was encouraged to make a second imression of three thousand copies, which also was nearly exhausted in a very short time. I consider myself amply rewarded for all my labours and pains by this manifestation of eagerness on the part of the public.

It is a great satisfaction to me that many persons, both mere men of the world as well as professors of Sastras, have not only condescended to publish replies to my work, but have spared no labour and expense on a subject which, I feared, would meet with their contempt and derision. It adds no little to my satisfaction to find that, among the replicants there are many, who are distinguished in this country for their rank, fortune and learning. What a piece of good fortune to me and to my little work, that such personages have deemed it worth their perusal, worth their discussion and worth being replied to.

But it is much to be regretted that, most of my replicants are not well acquainted with the manner in which such questions should be discussed. Some have been so infuriated at the very sound of the marriage of Widows, that they have lost all control over themselves; and their replies furnish instances of want of proper attention to the investigation of truth, arising from loss of temper during a controversy. Others, again, have wilfully avoided all discussion as to the merits of the question, and raised a number of false and futile objections. Their object, however, in so doing, has, in some measure, been gained. The generality of our countrymen, being ignorant of the Sastras, are incapable of arriving at the truth in any subject by weighing the arguments and authorities adduced and cited by two parties engaged in a Sastric controversy. The appearance of any objection, however futile, is apt to cast them into doubt and uncertainty. Many, who on perusal of my work came to the conclusion that the question agitated by me was consonant to the Sastras, soon after, jumped to the opposite conclusion, on finding a few objections started against it. The great majority of my countrymen, moreover, being ignorant of the Sanskrit language, cannot of themselves understand the meaning and spirit of Sanskrit Texts, which can only be made intelligible to them by vernacular translations, upon which they entirely depend, in order to ascertain the truth in an enquiry of this nature. Many of the replicants have availed themselves of this circumstance to subserve their purpose, by distorting the meaning of the Texts, cited by them in their respective works, and such readers, as are ignorant of the Sanskrit, have taken their interpretation to be the genuine version. For this, however, the readers are not to blame; for, no one can easily bring himself to believe, that any person, engaged in a religious controversy, would, by ingenious artifices and subterfuges, give wrong interpretation to the sayings of the sages, and, readily and without scruple or hesitation, publish them for the information of the public.

It is much more to be regretted, that many among the replicants delight in ridicule and are fond of abuse. I was not aware that, ridicule and abuse form the chief elements of a religious controversy in this country. Instead, however, of having recourse to abuse and ridicule, the replicants should have adopted the course which suits the importance of the subject. It is surprising that, with many, the reception of these antagonist pamphlets has been in exact proportion to the railing and personalities they contain. I was at first much aggrieved at the course, adopted by many of the replicants; but the perusal of a certain pamphlet has relieved me from all painful sensations. The reply is an annonymous one, under the signature of Vara (Bridegroom) who, though striken in years and every where reputed to be the wisest man in this part of the country, has, in several parts of his work, betrayed a fondness for scoffing and scurrilous jests. I have, therefore, come to the conclusion that, in a religious controversy, the use of ridicule and abusive language towards an adversary is the criterion of a wise man in this country. Had this been otherwise, the worthy and revered old man, whom the whole country unanimously pronounces to be the wisest, would not have adopted that course.

But whatever might be the character of the replies, I acknowledge my great obligations to their authors, and loudly offer them a thousand thanks. Had they not taken the trouble to reply to my work, it would have appeared that the learned and the influential portion of the community considered it beneath their notice. But it is, at least, clear from the replies that the subject, I have proposed, is not such as could be passed over with contempt and disregard. Their silence would, indeed, have been most mortifying to me. They have employed considerable labour and research in citing, in their respective works, all available arguments and authorities that could be adduced to prove, as they supposed, the nonconformity of the question to the Sastras. When, therefore, different persons have, in different ways, done their best to raise various objections against the marriage of Widows, it may be inferred that all that could be said against it has been exhausted. When these objections are weighed and examined, all doubts as to the consonance or otherwise of the practice of the marriage of widows to the Sastras, in the Kali-yuga, might be removed.

My adversaries have, in their respective works, written a great many things, but all of them are not relevant to the question at issue. I have, therefore, engaged myself to answer such of them as have appeared to me to have any bearing on the subject. As I have spared no pains and care in the framing of this answer, I humbly beseech my readers, that they would condescend to peruse this work once at least, from the beginning to the end, and I would consider all my labours amply rewarded.

CHAPTER I.

THE TEXT OF PARASARA APPLIES TO FEMALES ACTUALLY MARRIED, NOT TO VIRGINS MERELY BETROTHED.

Some have decided that the Text of Parasara, relative to marriage, purports to enjoin the marriage of a betrothed girl and not of a wedded woman, in the event of "No tidings being received of her husband &c. &c." It is necessary to consider, whether the decision of my opponents is correct.

Parasara says,

नष्टे मृते प्रव्रजिते क्लीबे च पतिते पतौ ।
पञ्चस्वापत्सु नारीणां पतिरन्यो विधीयते ॥

"On receiving no tidings of a husband, on his demise, on "his turning an ascetic, on his being found impotent, or on "his degradation, under any one of these five calamities, it "is canonical for women to take another husband."

The Text, understood according to the true meaning of the words used by Parasara, would naturally lead to the conclusion, that a woman can remarry under any one of the five calamities enumerated. No other conclusion can be arrived at, except by a forced interpretation of those words. Such interpretation is not however admissible, unless there be strong reasons for it. But no such reasons exist in this case, and therefore, Madhavacharya the Commentator, though antagonistic to the remarrying of females, has distinctly admitted that the Text of Parasara authorizes such remarriage, under the calamities aforesaid. Thus :—

परिवेदनपर्य्याधानयोरिव स्त्रीणां पुनरुद्वाहस्यापि
प्रसङ्गात् क्वचिदभ्यनुज्ञां दर्शयति

"Parasara, having treated of Parivodana,* and of Paryadhana,† shews that under certain circumstances the remarriage of women is lawful. Thus:—

नष्टे मृते प्रव्रजिते क्लीबे च पतिते पतौ।
पञ्चस्वापत्सु नारीणां पतिरन्यो विधीयते॥

* If the younger brother marries before the elder brother is married, that marriage is called *Parivedana*.

† If the younger brother consecrates fire before the elder brother does so, that act is called *Paryadhana*.

" On receiving no tidings of a husband, on his demise, on " his turning an ascetic, on his being found impotent, or on " his degradation, under any one of these five calamities, it " is canonical for women to take another husband."

पुनरुद्वाहमकृत्वा ब्रह्मचर्य्यव्रतानुष्ठाने श्रेयोऽतिशयं दर्शयति

" He next shows that it is more meritorious for women, to " observe the Brahmacharya than to marry again. Thus :—

मृते भर्त्तरि या नारी ब्रह्मचर्य्ये व्यवस्थिता ।
सा मृता लभते स्वर्गं यथा ते ब्रह्मचारिणः ॥

" That woman, who, on the decease of her husband, ob- " serves the Brahmacharya, attains heaven after her death."

ब्रह्मचर्य्यादप्यधिकं फलमनुगमने दर्शयति

" He then shows that concremation is attended with a " greater degree of merit than that attained from the ob- " servance of the Brahmacharya. Thus :—

तिस्रः कोट्योऽर्द्धकोटी च यानि लोमानि मानवे ।
तावत् कालं वसेत् स्वर्गं भर्त्तारं यानुगच्छति ॥

" She, who burns herself with her deceased husband, " resides in heaven for as many Kalas or thousands of years, " as there are hairs on the human body, or thirty five millions " of years."

On referring to the Narada Sanhita, it will be perfectly clear, that the injunction for remarriage as expressed in the Text, "On receiving no tidings of a husband &c. &c.," can by no means be applied to the case of a betrothed virgin. Thus :—

नष्टे मृते प्रव्रजिते क्लीबे च पतिते पतौ ।
पञ्चस्वापत्सु नारीणां पतिरन्यो विधीयते ॥
अष्टौ वर्षाण्युदीक्षेत ब्राह्मणी प्रोषितं पतिम् ।
अप्रसूता तु चत्वारि परतोऽन्यं समाश्रयेत् ॥
क्षत्रिया षट् समास्तिष्ठेदप्रसूता समात्रयम् ।
वैश्या प्रसूता चत्वारि द्वे वर्षे त्वितरा वसेत् ॥
न शूद्रायाः स्मृतः काल एष प्रोषितयोषिताम् ।
जीवति श्रूयमाणे तु स्यादेष द्विगुणो विधिः ॥
अप्रवृत्तौ तु भूतानां दृष्टिरेषा प्रजापतेः ॥
अतोऽन्यगमने स्त्रीणामेष दोषो न विद्यते" ॥

"On receiving no tidings of a husband, on his demise, on "his turning an ascetic, on his being found impotent, or on "his degradation, under any one of these five calamities, "it is canonical for women to take another husband. A "Brahmana woman should wait eight years for her absent "lord, and four years only, if she be childless ; then let her "marry again. A Kshatriya woman should wait six years, "and, in case she has no issue, three years only. A Vaisya "woman, if she has borne a child, four years, otherwise only "two. For a Sudra woman no period is mentioned for "which she is to wait for her husband. If it be heard "that he is living, the rule is, that the aforesaid periods are "to be doubled ; when tidings are not received, the fore-

* Narada Sanhita, Ch. XII.

"mentioned periods are enjoined. Such is the opinion of "Brahma, the lord of men. In such cases, therefore, there "is no harm in women marrying again."

It will now appear that, the aforesaid nuptial Text can, by no means, apply to a betrothed girl. In the case of an absent lord, different periods are assigned for which the wife is to wait for him, according as she has or has not any children. If this ordinance referred to a plighted virgin, the mention of the circumstance of her having or not having issue would be absurd. It may be urged that the Narada-sanhita was good only for the Satya-yuga, and therefore the Text quoted above cannot be construed to sanction the remarriage of women in the Kali-yuga, even if it were admitted that it enjoined such remarriage. It is true that the Narada-sanhita was good for the Satya-yuga, but the Text alluded to is identical with that of Parasara, both being composed of the same words. When both the Texts are identical, the meaning they convey cannot but be identical also. It would be absurd to assume that a particular set of words would mean one thing in one Yuga, and another thing in another Yuga. It is clear, therefore, that the Text can, on no account, have reference to the case of betrothed girls.

Those, who attempt to interpret the above Text of Parasara, as applying to the case of a betrothed girl and not to a married woman, do so for the following reason : There are some Texts which prohibit the marriage of wedded women, and if Parasara's Text be admitted to apply to married women, a discrepancy arises between the Texts. There are other Texts again which prescribe marriage for betrothed virgins, and if Parasara's Text be interpreted to apply to them, no discrepancy would occur. They therefore contend that Parasara's Text should be interpreted as having reference to betrothed girls only. But I must remark, that as there are Texts prohibitory of the marriage of wedded women, so the Text of Kasyapa prohibits the nuptials of a betrothed girl. Thus :—

सप्त पौनर्भवाः कन्या वर्ज्जनीयाः कुलाधमाः ।
वाचा दत्ता मनोदत्ता कृतकौतुकमङ्गला ।
उदकस्पर्शिता या च या च पाणिगृहीतिका ।
अग्निं परिगता या च पुनर्भूप्रभवा च या ।
इत्येताः काश्यपेनोक्ता दहन्ति कुलमग्निवत् ॥

"In forming a matrimonial connexion, seven Paunarbhava "damsels, despised of their families, are to be shunned. "The Vagdatta, she who has been plighted by words of "troth; the Manodatta, she whom her parent or guardian "has disposed of in his mind; the Krita-kautuka-mangala, "she on whose hand the nuptial string has been tied; the "Udaka-sparsita, she who has been given away by the "sprinkling of water; the Panigrihita, she in respect of "whom the ceremony of taking the hand has been performed; "the Agnim-parigata, she in respect of whom the marriage "ceremonies have been completed; the Punarbhu-pra-"bhava, she who is born of a Punarbhu; these seven dam-"sels, described by Kasyapa, when married, consume, like "fire, the family of their husbands."

Mark now, as Kasyapa includes the betrothed girl among those, who are to be shunned in marriage, and gives her the designation of Punarbhu (remarried), her marriage is necessarily interdicted. Kasyapa enjoins, that the betrothed girl and the married woman are equally to be rejected. If, therefore, the circumstance of some Texts prohibiting the marriage of a wedded woman be made to operate against the interpretation of the aforesaid Text of Parasara, as enjoining her remarriage; then, by parity of reasoning, that Text cannot be interpreted to apply to the case of a betrothed girl, when there is a prohibition in the Text of Kasyapa against it. Hence, the construction of the Texts of Parasara, as applying to the case of a betrothed girl, does not establish its consonancy with all the Texts of our Sastras on the subject. This is not, however, the way to reconcile all the Texts. If such reconciliation be necessary, it can be done in the following manner :

There is no mention in the Texts of Kasyapa and others, containing prohibition or injunction regarding the marriage of wedded women, of the specific Yugas to which they refer : hence, they should be considered applicable to all the Yugas. But when, in respect of the present question, there are certain ordinances or interdictions expressly laid down for the Kali-yuga, they may be said to be special rules appropriate to that Yuga only. And as distinct specific rules for the Kali-yuga, touching the present subject, are found, it is quite unnecessary to attempt to reconcile them with general rules regarding it. For, it is patent to all understandings, that a specific rule supersedes a general rule. It is therefore necessary that, all special rules relative to the Kali-yuga should be reconciled with each other, and upon such reconciliation depends the legality or otherwise of the marriage of widows in that Yuga. With this view, I here quote first such Texts, as prohibit the remarriage of women in the Kali-yuga:

Adi Purana.

ऊढायाः पुनरुद्वाहं ज्येष्ठांशं गोवधं तथा।
कलौ पञ्च न कुर्वीत भ्रातृजायां कमण्डलुम् *॥

"The remarriage of a married woman, the giving of the "best share to the eldest brother, the slaughter of a cow, "procreation on a brother's wife, turning an ascetic, these "five acts are not to be performed in the Kali-yuga."

Kratu.

देवराच्च सुतोत्पत्तिर्दत्ता कन्या प्रदीयते।
न यज्ञे गोवधः कार्यः कलौ न च कमण्डलुः॥

"In the Kali-yuga, the brother is not to beget a child on "a brother's wife, a girl already given is not to be given "away, a cow is not to be slaughtered in religious ceremonies, "and no one is to turn an ascetic.

Vrihannaradiya Purana.

दत्तायाश्चैव कन्यायाः पुनर्दानं परस्य च।

* Quoted by Madhavacharya in his commentary on the Parasara Sanhita.

" In the Kali-yuga, a damsel is not to be given to a bride-
" groom a second time."

Aditya Purana.

दत्ता कन्या प्रदीयते ।

" In the Kali-yuga, the gift of a girl already given is for-
" bidden."

Thus there is, in general terms, a prohibition of the remarriage of women in the Adi Purana, the Kratu Sanhita, and the Aditya and Vrihânnaradiya Puranas. But in the Parasara Sanhita we find,

नष्टे मृते प्रव्रजिते क्लीबे च पतिते पतौ ।
पञ्चस्वापत्सु नारीणां पतिरन्यो विधीयते ॥

" On receiving no tidings of a husband, on his demise, on
" his turning an ascetic, on his being found impotent, or
" on his degradation, under any one of these five calamities,
" it is canonical for women to take another husband."

That is, under any of these five contingencies, the remarriage of a woman is permitted.

Thus, we have now before us Texts both for and against the remarriage of women in the Kali-yuga. If we attempt to reconcile these apparently contradictory Texts, we should do so in the following manner:

In the Adi Purana and the other works, quoted above, the prohibition against the marriage of wedded women in the Kali-yuga is a general one; but Parasara makes special cases under five different contingencies, in which such marriage is permitted. Where there are both a general and a special rule regarding a particular subject, the usual course is to apply the latter to the exceptional cases, and to adopt the former in all other cases. Hence it follows that the precept of Parasara should be observed in the five special contingencies mentioned, the prohibition in the Adi Purana &c. being strictly adhered to in all other cases. This interpretation reconciles the two apparently contradictory classes of Texts, and affords room for the application of both the precept and the prohibition. Let us enter into a detailed examination of the subject.

Katyayana says—

स तु यद्यन्यजातीयः पतितः क्लीब एव वा।
विकर्मस्थः सगोत्रो वा दासो दीर्घामयोऽपि वा।
ऊढापि देया सान्यस्मै सहाभरणभूषणा॥*

"If after wedding, the husband be found to be of a "different caste, degraded, impotent, unprincipled, of the "same Gotra or family a slave, or a valitudinarian, then a "married woman should be bestowed upon another, decked "with proper apparel and ornaments."

Vasishtha says—

कुलशीलविहीनस्य षण्ढादिपतितस्य च।
अपस्मारिविधर्मस्य रोगिणां वेषधारिणाम्॥
दत्तामपि हरेत् कन्यां सगोत्रोढां तथैव च॥†

* Katyayana, quoted in the Parasara Bhashya and Nirnaya Sindhu.

† Vasishtha, quoted in the Udvahatattwa.

"A girl, married to a person who is of a low family and "conduct, impotent, degraded, epileptic, unprincipled, sickly, "a devotee, or of the same family, is to be taken away from "him, that is, married to another."

Narada says—

नष्टे मृते प्रव्रजिते क्लीबे च पतिते पतौ।
पञ्चस्वापत्सु नारीणां पतिरन्यो विधीयते॥

"On receiving no tidings of a husband, on his demise, on "his turning an ascetic, on his being found impotent, or on "his degradation, under any one of these five calamities, it is "canonical for women to take another husband."

Thus, Katyayana, vasishtha and Narada, without alluding to any particular Yuga, have generally enjoined the remarriage of a woman when her husband is unprincipled, degraded, impotent, sickly, epileptic, of low family and conduct, an ascetic, a slave, of the same family, of a different caste, when no tidings are received of him, or when dead.

Adi Purana says—

ऊढायाः पुनरुद्वाहं ज्येष्ठांशं गोवधं तथा।
कलौ पञ्च न कुर्वीत भ्रातृजायां कमण्डलुम्॥

"The remarriage of a married woman, the giving of the "best share to the eldest brother, the slaughter of a cow, "procreation on a brother's wife, or turning an ascetic, these "five acts are not to be performed in the Kali-yuga."

Krutu says—

देवराच्च सुतोत्पत्तिर्दत्ता कन्या न दीयते।
न यज्ञे गोवधः कार्य्यः कलौ नच कमण्डलुः॥

"In the Kali-yuga, the brother is not to beget a child "on a brother's wife, a girl already given is not to be given "away, a cow is not to be slaughtered in religious cere-"monies, and no one is to turn an ascetic."

Vrihannaradiya Purana says—

दत्तायाश्चैव कन्यायाः पुनर्दानं परस्य च।

"In the Kali-yuga, a damsel is not to be given to a bride-"groom a second time."

Aditya Purana says—

दत्ता कन्या प्रदीयते।

"In the Kali-yuga, the gift of a girl already given is "forbidden."

But the Parasara Sanhita says—

नष्टे मृते प्रव्रजिते क्लीबे च पतिते पतौ।
पञ्चस्वापत्सु नारीणां पतिरन्यो विधीयते॥

"On receiving no tidings of a husband, on his demise, "on his turning an ascetic, on his being found impotent, or "on his degradation, under any one of these five calamities "it is canonical for women to take another husband."

Thus, the Adi Purana and other works, in general terms, prohibit the remarriage of wedded women in the Kali-yuga; while Parasara specially enjoins such marriage in the Kali-yuga, under the five circumstances specified by him.

Now, let my readers consider that Katyayana and other Sages, without alluding to any particular Yuga, enumerate certain cases, in which they enjoin the remarriage of a wedded woman. Such a rule would have answered for all the Yugas ; but as in the Adi Purana and other works such marriage has been forbidden in the Kali-yuga, the prohibition is special to that Yuga : hence, the ordinances of Katyayana and others apply to the three Yugas other than the Kali.

Again, in the Adi Purana and other works, the remarriage of women in the Kali-yuga has been generally prohibited, without the specification of any exceptional cases ; but Parasara points out particular conditions, under which he declares such marriage in that Yuga to be canonical. The injunction of Parasara, therefore, is a special rule ; and the general prohibition in the Adi Purana and other works apply to all but the five cases specified by Parasara.

Such is always the case, when there are both general and special injunctions or prohibitions on the same subject. Thus :—

অহরহঃ সন্ধ্যামুপাসীত।

"Day by day the Sandhya (a ceremony) is to be performed."

This is a clear general rule, for the performance of the Sandhya laid down in the Vedas. But,

सन्ध्यां पञ्च महायज्ञान् नैत्यकं स्मृतिकर्म्म च ।
तन्मध्ये हापयेत्तेषां दशाहान्ते पुनः क्रिया ॥*

"The Sandhya, the five great sacrifices, and the daily "necessary rites, enjoined by the Smritis, are not to be per- "formed during the period of Asaucha (impurity); after the "expiration of that period, they are to be performed again."

Here, Javali prohibits the performance of the Sandhya, during the period of Asaucha. Now mark, though there is a general ordinance in the Vedas for the daily performance of the Sandhya, yet it is not performed during the period of Asaucha, by the special prohibition of Javali. Again,

पूर्व्वां सन्ध्यां जपंस्तिष्ठेत् सावित्रीमार्कदर्शनात् ।
पश्चिमान्तु समासीनः सम्यगृक्षविभावनात् ॥ 101.
न तिष्ठति तु यः पूर्व्वां नोपास्ते यस्तु पश्चिमाम् ।
स शूद्रवद्बहिष्कार्य्यः सर्व्वस्माद्द्विजकर्म्मणः ॥ 103. †

"At the morning twilight, let him (a twice-born) stand "repeating the Gayatri, until he sees the sun; and at the "evening twilight, let him repeat it sitting, until the stars "distinctly appear. But he, who stands not repeating in the "morning twilight, and sits not repeating in the evening, "must be precluded, like a Sudra, from every sacred obser- "vance of the twice-born classes." But,

* Javali, quoted in the Suddhitattwa.

† Manu. Ch. II.

संक्रान्त्यां पक्षयोरन्ते द्वादश्यां श्राद्धवासरे ।
सायं सन्ध्यां न कुर्वीत कृते च पितृहा भवेत् ॥*

"On the day of the passage of the sun to a new Zodiacal "sign, on the last day of either half of the lunar month, "on the twelfth as well as twenty-seventh day of the moon, "and on the day of the celebration of a Shraddha, the "Sandhya is not to be performed in the evening; by doing "so the sin of parricide is incurred."

Observe now, in spite of the general injunction in the institutes of Manu for the performance of the Sandhya in the morning and evening and the penalty attached to its violation, it is not performed on certain specified days by the special prohibition of Vyasa; that is, the general injunction for the performance of the Sandhya obtains on days other than those specified by that Sage. In the Vedas is the following prohibition—

मा हिंस्यात् सर्वभूतानि ।

"Kill no living thing."

But in other places of the Vedas there are such injunctions as the following—

अश्वमेधेन यजेत ।

"This sacrifice is to be performed by the slaughter of a "horse."

पशुना रुद्रं यजेत ।

* Vyasa, quoted in the Tithitattwa.

"The sacrifice, called the Rudra-yaga, is to be performed "by the slaughter of cattle."

अग्नीषोमीयं पशुमालभेत।

"The sacrifice in honor of Agni and Soma is to be per- "formed by the slaughter of cattle."

वायव्यं श्वेतमालभेत।

"The sacrifice in honor of Vayu is to be performed by "the slaughter of a white goat."

Now mark, despite the most clear and positive general prohibition, in one part of the Vedas, against killing animals, their slaughter, in certain sacrifices, is considered a meritorious act by the special injunctions in other parts of the Vedas; that is, owing to the special injunction, the general prohibition, against the slaughter of animals, is applicable to all cases except those of the equine sacrifice, the Rudra-yaga and the like. On this account the illustrious Manu has said—

मधुपर्के च यज्ञे च पितृदैवतकर्म्मणि।
अत्रैव पशवो हिंस्या नान्यत्रेत्यब्रवीन्मनुः॥ 5. 41.

"On a solemn offering to a guest, at a sacrifice, and in "holy rites to the manes or to the gods, on these occasions "only and not in others, may cattle be slain; this law Manu "has enacted."

It should be observed, that in the above cited cases, our acts are guided by special rules in spite of general ones to the contrary; the latter obtaining force only in cases not comprehended in the former. In spite, then, of the general prohibition against the remarriage of women in the Kali-yuga, the special ordinance of Parasara, directing their remarriage under the five conditions specified by him, is to be observed; the general prohibition in the Adi Purana and other works obtaining force in all cases except those five. This I consider to be the plain and rational way of reconciling apparently contradictory Texts on the subject under discussion.

CHAPTER II.

THE MARITAL TEXT OF PARASARA REFERS TO THE KALI-YUGA, NOT TO THE OTHER YUGAS.

Madhavacharya, after giving an interpretation of the Text of Parasara respecting the remarriage of females, thus concludes,—

अयञ्च पुनरुद्वाहो युगान्तरविषयः। तथाचादिपुराणम्

ऊढायाः पुनरुद्वाहं ज्येष्ठांशं गोवधं तथा।

कलौ पञ्च न कुर्वीत भ्रातृजायां कमण्डलुम्॥

"This injunction of Parasara, for the remarriage of "females, is to be understood to apply to Yugas other than "the Kali; because it is declared, in the Adi Purana, that the "remarriage of a female once wedded, the allotment of the "best share to the eldest brother, the Bovine sacrifice, pro-

"creation on a brother's wife, and turning an ascetic, are the "five acts not to be practised in the Kali-yuga."

It should now be considered, whether this remark of Madhavacharya is correct and reasonable. It is necessary, in the first place, to ascertain the object of Parasara from the spirit of his Sanhita and its interpretation by Madhavacharya himself.

The Text of the Sanhita.

अथातो हिमशैलाग्रे देवदारुवनालये ।
व्यासमेकाग्रमासीनमपृच्छन्नृषयः पुरा ॥
मानुषाणां हितं धर्म्मं वर्त्तमाने कलौ युगे ।
शौचाचारं यथावच्च वद सत्यवतीसुत ॥

"*Therefore*, in times of yore, the Rishis, *thereafter*, addressed Vyasa—who was seated, with his attention fixed on one "object, in his retreat in the pine forests on the top of the "Himalayas.—Declare to us, Oh son of Satyavati! what "are the Dharmas (duties) and acharas (practices) beneficial "to men in this Kali-yuga."

Commentary of Madhavacharya.

वर्त्तमाने कलाविति विशेषणात् युगान्तरधर्म्मश्रवणानन्तर्य्यम् ।

"*Thereafter*, that is, the Rishis, after having been informed "of the Dharmas of the Satya, Treta, and Dwapara Yugas, "enquired about the Dharmas of the Kali-yuga."

अतःप्रश्नो हेतवः यथादेशदेशाख्यायिनो नायेषधर्म्माणां
यथाश्च युगान्तरधर्म्मश्रवणात्र न कलिधर्म्मविषमतिस्वयमाहिति ।

"*Therefore*, that is, whereas the study of a part cannot "make one acquainted with the whole of the Dharmas, and "whereas the Kali Dharmas cannot be known from an ac-"quaintance with the Dharmas of other Yugas, therefore the "Rishis enquired."

From this it clearly appears, that at the commencement of the Kali-yuga, the Rishis, who knew the Dharmas of the Satya, Treta, and Dwapara Yugas, wishing to obtain a knowledge of those for the Kali-yuga, repaired to Vyasa and questioned him on the subject.

Text.

तच्छ्रुत्वा ऋषिवाक्यन्तु सशिष्योऽग्न्यर्कसन्निभः ।
प्रत्युवाच महातेजाः श्रुतिस्मृतिविशारदः ॥
न चाहं सर्वतत्त्वज्ञः कथं धर्म्मं वदाम्यहम् ।
अस्मत्पितैव प्रष्टव्य इति व्यासः सुतोऽवदत् ॥

"Hearing those words of the Rishis, he (the great Vaysa), "surrounded by his pupils, radiant as the sun and fire, and "versed in the Vedas and the Smritis, replied, *I do not know* "*the truth of all things*, how shall I declare the Dharmas? "*My father only should be consulted on the subject*. This was "said by the son of Parasara."

Commentary.

न चाहमिति वदतो व्यासस्यायमाशयः यद्यपि कलिधर्म्माः पृच्छ्यन्ते तत्र न तावदहं ज्ञातः कलिधर्म्मतत्त्वं जानामि अस्मत्पितुरेव तत्र प्रावीण्यात् अतएव कलौ पाराशराः स्मृता इति वक्ष्यते । यदि

पितृप्रसादाज्जानामि तदभिज्ञानं तस्मिंश्च एव पिता प्रष्टव्यः सति हि मूल-वक्तरि विद्यमाने प्रश्नक्रिया युज्यत इति।

"*I do dot know &c.* by this, Vyasa means to say that you "are now enquiring of me the Kali Dharmas; but I have "learnt them from my father; he only is master of them; "and as I have obtained a knowledge of them through my "father's favour, he should be consulted on the subject; "when the original instructor is living, it is not meet to re-"ceive knowledge at second hand."

एवकारेणान्यस्मृतिकर्त्तारो व्यावर्त्त्यन्ते। यद्यपि मन्वादयः कलिधर्म्माभिज्ञास्तथापि पराशरस्यास्मिन् विषये तपोविशेषवशात् असाधारणः कश्चिदतिशयो द्रष्टव्यः। यथा काण्वमाध्यन्दिनकाठककौथुमतैत्तिरीयादिशाखासु काण्वादीनामसाधारणत्वं तद्वदत्राप्यवगन्तव्यम्। कलिधर्म्मसम्प्रदायोपेतस्यापि पराशरसुतस्य यदा तदन्यं दृष्टाभिपदने सङ्कोचः तदा किमु वक्तव्यमन्येषामिति।

"From the expression *my father only should be consulted* "*on the subject* it is to be inferred, that the authors of the "other Smritis are excluded (as referees on this subject.) "Although Manu and others, are versed in the Kali Dhar-"mas, yet Parasara, by virtue of particular penances, has "become the supreme authority as regards the Kali Dharmas. "As among the Kanwa, Madhyandina, Kathaka, Kauthuma, "Taittiriya and other Sakhas or branches of the Vedas the "Kanwa and some others are distinguished, so, in respect "of the Kali Dharmas, Parasara stands preeminent among "all the authors of the Smritis. When Vyasa, who is him-"self admitted to be the instructor of the Kali Dharmas, "hesitates to declare them while Parasara is living, what "shall we say of the other Rishis."

We thus see that as regards the Kali Dharmas, the authority of Parasara weighs more than that of Manu and other writers of Smritis and that his Text is supreme on the subject of the Kali Dharmas.'

Text.

यदि जानासि मे भक्तिं स्नेहाद्वा भक्तवत्सल ।
धर्म्मं कथय मे तात अनुग्राह्यो ह्यहं तव ॥

"Oh Sir ! affectionate to thy votaries, if thou knowest "me to be thy votary and bearest any affection towards me, "instruct me in the Dharmas ; I am an object of thy "favour."

Vyasa thus addressed his father.

Commentary.

ननु सन्ति बहवो मन्वादिभिः प्रोक्ता धर्म्माः तत्र को धर्म्मो भवता बुभुत्सित इत्याशङ्क्य बुभुत्सितं परिशेषयितुमुपन्यस्यति

"There are various Dharmas promulgated by Manu and "others, and Vyasa, fearing as if Parasara asked him which "of them he wished to learn first, mentions the Dharmas in "which he has been already edified, that he may conclude "with specifying the Dharmas, he wishes to learn."

Text.

श्रुता मे मानवा धर्म्मा वासिष्ठाः काश्यपास्तथा ।
गार्गेया गौतमाश्चैव तथाचौशनसाः श्रुताः ॥
अत्रेर्विष्णोश्च सांवर्त्ता दाक्षा आङ्गिरसास्तथा ।
शातातपाश्च हारीता याज्ञवल्क्यास्तथैव च ॥
आपस्तम्बकृता धर्म्माः शङ्खस्य लिखितस्य च ।
कात्यायनकृताश्चैव प्राचेतसकृताश्च ये ॥
श्रुता ह्येते भवत्प्रोक्ताः श्रुतार्थास्ते न विस्मृताः ।
अस्मिन् मन्वन्तरे धर्म्माः कृतत्रेतादिके युगे ॥

"I have heard from you the Dharmas declared by Manu, "Vasishtha, Kasyapa, Garga, Gotama, Usana, Atri, Vishnu, "Sanvartta, Daksha, Angira, Satatapa, Harita, Yajnavalkya, "Apastamba, Saukha, Likhita, Katyayana, and Prachetasa. "I have not forgotten what I learnt; they were the Dharmas "of the Satya, Treta, and Dwapara Yugas."

Commentary.

इदानीं परिशिष्टं बुभुत्सितं पृच्छति

"And now he enquires about the Dharmas, he wishes "to learn."

Text.

सर्वे धर्म्माः कृते जाताः सर्वे नष्टाः कलौ युगे ।
चातुर्वर्ण्यसमाचारं किञ्चित् साधारणं वद ॥

"All the Dharmas originated in the Satya-yuga, all of "them have expired in the Kali-yuga: declare therefore "some of the common Dharmas of the four Varnas (castes)."

Commentary.

विष्णुपुराणे

वर्णाश्रमाचाररता प्रवृत्तिर्न कलौ नृणाम्।

आदिपुराणेऽपि

यस्तु कार्त्तयुगे धर्म्मो न कर्त्तव्यः कलौ युगे।

पापप्रसक्तास्तु यतः कलौ नार्य्यो नरास्तथा॥

अतः कलौ प्राणिनां प्रयासबाहुल्ये धर्म्मे प्रवृत्त्यसम्भवात् सुकरो धर्म्मोऽत्र बुभुत्सितः।

"It is said in the Vishnu Purana that 'the specified Dhar-
"mas of the four Varnas (castes) and of the four Asramas
"(orders,) are not observed in the Kali-yuga.' It is also
"declared in the Adi Purana that 'the Dharmas of the Satya
"Yuga cannot be practised in the Kali-yuga; because both
"men and women, all, are addicted to sin.' Men in the
"Kali-yuga cannot be expected to have any predilection for
"Dharmas, which are difficult to be practised: the incul-
"cation of the easily practicable Dharmas, therefore, is the
"object of the Parasara Sanhita."

By all this, it is manifest that the Dharmas, inculcated by Manu and others, are appropriate to the Satya, Treta and Dwapara Yugas, and that the observance of all of them in the Kali-yuga is impracticable. Vyasa, therefore, asks of Parasara for such Dharmas as are easily performable in the Kali-yuga.

Text.

व्यासवाक्यावसाने तु मुनिमुख्यः पराशरः।

धर्म्मस्य निर्णयं प्राह सूक्ष्मं स्थूलञ्च विस्तरात्॥

"On the conclusion of Vyasa's speech, Parasara, the chief "of Sages, began to propound, in detail, the general prin-"ciples and subtle points of the Dharmas."

Thus it appears, that, at the request of Vyasa, Parasara, who tenderly loved his son, began to declare the Dharmas of the Kali-yuga.

Now let my readers calmly think, whether or not, the above citations of the Texts of Parasara and of the commentary of Madhavacharya himself clearly and unquestionably prove, that the sole object of the Parasara Sanhita is the inculcation of the Dharmas of the Kali-yuga. When it is understood that such is the object of the work, it must be acknowledged that the whole work, from beginning to end, has reference to the Kali-yuga only. It would, therefore, be absurd to suppose that the Text relative to the marriage of widows and other women applies to the other Yugas. How can it be reasonably supposed that when Vyasa and other Sages, at the commencement of the Kali-yuga, distinctly declare their having acquired a knowledge of the Dharmas of the preceding Yugas, and therefore ask Parasara to edify them in the Dharmas of the Kali-yuga, he would, in inculcating the Dharmas of that Yuga throughout his work, prescribe only a single Dharma which applies to Yugas other than the Kali. There can be no doubt, therefore, that Parasara has prescribed the remarriage of women as a Dharma appropriate to the Kali-yuga.

It has been shewn above that Madhavacharya has, in his own interpretation, decided that the object of the

Parasara Sanhita is the propounding of the Kali Dharmas. Any conclusion therefore arrived at by the Commentator, which is contrary to the scope of the Sanhita and opposed to his own interpretation, can never be accepted as rational.

Madhavacharya's gloss, to the following effect, on the three Texts of Parasara relative to remarriage, Brahmacharya, and concremation, becomes incoherent, if the Text relative to remarriage be supposed to refer to Yugas other than the Kali:

"Under cartain contingencies the remarriage of a woman "is legal."

"It is more meritorious for a woman who, instead of "marrying again, observes the Brahmacharya."

"Concremation is attended with a greater degree of merit "than what is attained from the observance of Brahma- "charya."

In the opinion of Madhávacharya, remarriage refers to the prior Yugas ; Brahmacharya and concremation to the Kali-yuga. There can be therefore no connexion between the Text which speaks of remarriage and those which direct Brahmacharya and concremation. Now, when Madhavacharya, by deciding that the marital Text refers to the former Yugas, leaves not to the widows of the Kali-yuga, any right to remarriage, the idea of comparison, expressed in the Text which promises higher rewards to the widow of the Kali-yuga who, instead of marrying, observes the Brahmacharya, would be quite absurd. The obvious connexion subsisting between the three Texts, which declare in the first place, remarriage of women to be canonical; secondly, the observance of the Brahamacharya to be instrumental in procuring greater merit; and thirdly, concremation to be the passport to still higher rewards; inevitably leads to the conclusion, that these three injunctions apply to one and the same Yuga: If remarriage be considered to refer to the preceding Yugas, Brahmacharya and concremation must necessarily be deemed appropriate to those Yugas; and if the latter two be viewed as assigned for the Kali-yuga, the former must also apply to this Yuga. Want of mutual connexion would destroy the sense. It must be confessed, in short, that Madhavacharya, in his zeal to reckon the marriage of widows among the Dharmas of the former Yugas, has not only strayed from the obvious purport of the author of the Sanhita, but has neglected to see, whether this dictum would tally with his own interpretation of the passage.

Madhavacharya has himself declared that 'as it is not expected that men in the Kali yuga would have any predilection for the Dharmas which are difficult to be observed, it is the object of Parasara to assign such Dharmas for the Kali-yuga, as are easily practicable.' Considering remarriage to be a Dharma easily practicable, Parasara has, in the first place, laid it down as a Dharma for the widows in general. Secondly, the observance of the Brahmacharya being a difficult task, he has enjoined it for those women who feel their strength equal to it, declaring that its observance would be a passport to heaven. Thirdly, concremation being the severest duty, he has ordained it for those women whose courage is commensurate with the task, by encouraging them with the hope of eternal residence in heaven. Madhavacharya has however reckoned the easily practicable duty of remarriage as a Dharma of the past yugas, and assigned the remaining two most arduous duties only (Brahmacharya and concremation) as appropriate to the Kali-yuga. Now, let my readers consider, whether this allotment of Madhavacharya squares with his former exposition, that men in the Kali-yuga not being disposed to observe the Dharmas which are difficult of performance, the avowed object of Parasara is the assignment of the easily practicable Dharmas for men of the Kali-yuga. It is certainly a strange hypothesis that a most easily practicable Dharma, which the strong minded men of the byegone ages were privileged to perform, should have been interdicted to a feeble and degenerate race. In fact, when it is considered that the people of the Kali-yuga have immeasurably fallen off, in their physical and moral strength, from their ancestors of the prior Yugas, and are therefore incapable of practising the difficult Dharmas ; when parasara, having commenced declaring the Dharmas of the Kali-yuga has, in respect of widows in general, ordained, in the first instance, remarriage the most easily practicable Dharma, we come to the irresistible conclusion that Madhavacharya's supposition of remarriage not being intended for the widows of the Kali-yuga can never be reconciled with reason or the avowed object of the author of the Sanhita.

That the above interpretation of Madhavacharya is opposed to the intention of Parasara is clearly evident also from the writings of Bhattojidikshita, who thus declares his opinion :

न च कलिनिषिद्धस्यापि युगान्तरीयधर्म्मस्यैव नष्टे मृते इत्यादिपराशरवाक्यं प्रतिपादकमिति वाच्यं कलावनुष्ठेयान् धर्म्मानेव वक्ष्यामीति प्रतिज्ञाय तद्ग्रन्थप्रणयनात्।"

" It cannot be contended that the Marital Text of Para-
" sara applies to Yugas other than the Kali, for Parasara
" has compiled his Sanhita, with the avowed object of
" declaring the Dharmas to be observed in the Kali-yuga
" alone."

From the arguments and citations above set-forth, the nonconsonancy of the interpretation of Madhavacharya to the scope of the Parasara-sanhita and to his own exposition of the three Texts relating to remarriage, Brahmacharya, and concremation, has been sufficiently establishd. We should now examine the weight of the authority, on the strength of which he founds his supposition that remarriage was not intended for the Kali-yuga.

Madhavacharya, in attempting to refer the remarriage of females to Yugas other than the Kali, has not been able to derive any support either from the general scope of the Sanhita or from the obvious meaning and construction of the Text in question, but has suffered himself to be guided by a single Text of the Adi Purana. His meaning seems to be this : although the Parasara

Chaturvinsati Smriti Vyakhya. Section on marriage.

Sanhita is appropriate to the Kali-yuga only and although it enjoins the remarriage of females, yet as there appears a prohibition in the Adi Purana against the remarriage of women once wedded, in the Kali-yuga, the injunction of Parasara should be considered not to refer to the Kali-yuga but to the preceding Yugas.

Three strong objections may be raised against this reasoning— Ist, The Text, which Madhavacharya declares to have cited from the Adi Purana, is not to be found in that Purana ; moreover, when regard is had to the scheme of the work, the improbability of any such Text being found in it would be manifest : the citation of Madhavacharya, therefore, appears to be unfounded, and any conclusion, which it supports, should be considered as unauthorized. Scondly, should the Text in question be admitted to be genuine, it is not reasonable to qualify, on its strength, the Text of Parasara ; for Parasara Sanhita is one of the Smritis and the Adi Purana is a Puranic work : and it has been clearly shewn * that in the event of a contradiction between the Smriti and the Purana, the former would be the stronger authority ; that is, we should, in that case, instead of following the injunctions of the Purana, act up to those of the Smriti. By this rule therefore no Text of a Smriti can be qualified by any Puranic Text, when they seem to jar with each other. In the third place, from what has been said in the preceding chapter respecting the cogency of special rules, we should, instead of suffering the

* See sage 18.

Text of the Adi Purana to qualify that of the Parasara Sanhita, rather reverse the process: The prohibition in the Adi Purana is a general rule, while Parasara's ordinance is a special one; the general rule, instead of barring the operation of a special rule, should be superseded by the latter. Mark now, the interpretation of Madhavacharya referring the injunction of Parasara for remarriage of females to Yugas other than the Kali, is—Firstly, opposed to the spirit and scope of the Sanhita; secondly, inconsistent with his own expositions; thirdly, founded on an authority, the genuineness of which is questionable; fourthly, (the genuineness of the authority being granted) contrary to the rule laid down by Vyasa which declares the authority of the Smriti to be superior to that of the Purana, when they are at variance with each other; and fifthly, contradictive to the universal doctrine that a special rule supersedes a general one. In fact the supposition that the marital Text of Parasara refers to Yugas other than the Kali is untenable.

A fresh objection may start up: Madhavacharya was a great scholar; we should accept his doctrine without questioning its reasonableness. To this, I have only to observe, that Madhavacharya was, indeed, a learned man and, in all respects, highly venerated; but he was not infallible, nor are his opinions always accepted as infallible. Whenever his conclusions were unsound, succeeding writers have not scrupled to refute and criticize them. Thus:—

यत्तु माधवः सद्य मासपर्यन्तो स्यात् तच्च पक्षिविदिमाहुरा ।

न कार्यमाहितः किन्तु सदा वर्ज्यदिने हि या इत्याह तत् कर्कभाष्यदेवजानीश्रीअनन्तभाष्यादिसकलवाजसनेयिग्रन्थविरोधाद्बहूनामनादराच्चोपेक्ष्यम्। *

"What Madhavacharya has said here cannot be accept-
"ed as authoritative, because it is opposed to the Karka-
"bhashya, Devajani, Sri Anantabhashya and all other
"writers on the Vajasaneya Sakha, and disregaraded by
"many."

माधवस्तु सामान्यवाक्यान्निर्णयं कुर्वन् भ्रान्त एव। †

"Madhavacharya in attempting to settle the point, accord-
"ing to the common acceptation of the term, has entangled
"himself in the meshes of fallacy."

कृष्णा पूर्वोत्तरा युक्ता दशम्येवं व्यवस्थितेति माधवः। वस्तुतस्तु मुख्या नवमीयुतैव ग्राह्या। दशमी तु प्रकर्त्तव्या सद्गुर्वी द्विजसत्तमेत्यापस्तम्बोक्तेः। ‡

"Madhavacharya lays down this rule, but we must follow
"a different course."

मासि चाश्वयुजे शुक्ले नवरात्रे विशेषतः।
सम्पूज्य नवदुर्गाञ्च नक्तं कुर्यात् समाहितः।
नवरात्राभिधं कर्म्म नक्तव्रतमिदं स्मृतम्॥

आरम्भे नवरात्रस्येत्यादिस्कान्दात् माधवोक्तेश्च नक्तमेव प्रधानमिति चेत् न नवरात्रोपवासतः इत्यादेरनुपपत्तेः। §

* Nirnayasindhu. Ch. I. † Nirnayasindhu. Ch. II.

‡ Nirnayasindhu. Ch. I. § Nirnayasindhu. Ch. II.

"If you say that the rule is valid, because it has been "declared by Madhavacharya and is to be found in the Skanda "Purana, then the other Sastras are falsified."

यत्र मासमध्यादर्वाक् चतुर्दश्यौ समाप्तौ तदन्ते तदूर्ध्वं मासि-न्यायेन मासविशिष्टस्य एवेति हेमाद्रिमाधवादयो व्यवस्थामाहुः तन्न तिथ्यन्ते तिथिभान्ते वा पारणं यत्र चोदितम्। याम-त्रयोर्ध्वगामिन्यां प्रातरेव हि पारणेत्यादिवाक्यानामनवकाशत्वेन व्यवस्थाविधेरनवकाशविधवाक्यद्वयस्य दुष्परिहरत्वात्।*

"Hemadri, Madhavacharya and others have settled this "rule, but it should not be received; for then the conclusion "would be irresistible, that both the dicta are useless."

अथ यदि प्रथमनिशायामेवाष्टमीयोगस्तदापि ब्रह्मवैवर्तादि-वचनाद्दिवापारणमनन्तभट्टमाधवाचार्योक्तं युक्तमिति वाच्यं न रात्रौ पारणं कुर्य्यादृते वै रोहिणीव्रतात्। निशायां पारणं कुर्यात् वर्जयित्वा महानिशामिति संवत्सरप्रदीपधृतस्य न रात्रौ पारणं कुर्य्यादृते वै रोहिणीव्रतात्। अत्र निश्यपि तत्-कार्यं वर्जयित्वा महानिशामिति ब्रह्माण्डोक्तस्य च निर्विषय-त्वापत्तेः।†

"If you say that the conclusion arrived at by Ananta Bhat-"ta and Madhavacharya are valid, then the quotation in the "Sanvatsara Pradipa, and the Text of the Brahmanda Purana "will have no sphere of application."

Thus Kamalakarabhatta and Rughunandana have not

* Nirnayasindhu. ch. II. † Tithitattwa.

failed to refute his doctrines when they appeared open to objection : wherefore it clearly appears, that the dictum of Madhavacharya, right or wrong, is not to be received as an infallible authority.

CHAPTER III.

The marital injunction of Parasara is not opposed to Manu.

Almost all the oppositionists have come to the conclusion, that the marriage of widows is against the law of Manu ; whereby they mean to establish that the Text of Parasara, though it authorizes the marriage of widows in the Kali-yuga, being opposed to Manu, should be rejected on the strength of the following Text of Vrihaspati :

वेदार्थोपनिबन्धृत्वात् प्राधान्यं हि मनोः स्मृतम्।
मन्वर्थविपरीता या सा स्मृतिर्न प्रशस्यते॥ *

"Manu has, in his own Sanhita, compilod the spirit of the "Vedas ; he is, therefore, the chief authority ; and Smritis at "variance with him are not proper guides.

This conclusion does not appear to be rational. Vrihaspati directs that the Manu Sanhita is the chief authority,

* Quoted by Kulluka Bhatta.

and the Smritis at variance with it are to be rejected; but he does not specify any particular Yuga or Yugas in which that Sanhita is to be so regarded. On the other hand, Parasara, an equally wise and infallible Sage, distinctly affirms that the Sanhita of Manu was appropriate for the Satya-yuga only, and not for all the Yugas. The direction of Vrihaspati, in general terms, might have applied to all the Yugas as advanced by the oppositionists, if Parasara did not particularize the Satya-yuga. It must accordingly be admitted that the Sanhita of Manu was supreme authority in that Yuga only, and not in any other Yuga. That it is not so in the Kali-yuga, is also evident from the fact that, in many instances, the prevailing practices are founded on Smritis plainly at variance with that Sanhita. Thus.—

Manu has said—

त्रिंशद्वर्षो वहेत् कन्यां हृद्यां द्वादशवार्षिकीम्।
त्र्यष्टवर्षोऽष्टवर्षां वा धर्मे सीदति सत्वरः॥ 9. 94.

"A man, aged thirty years, is to marry a girl of twelve; or "a man of twenty-four years, a damsel of eight: a breach of "this rule makes a man sinful."

But Angira declares—

अष्टवर्षा भवेद्गौरी नववर्षा तु रोहिणी।
दशमे कन्यका प्रोक्ता अत ऊर्ध्वं रजस्वला॥
तस्मात् संवत्सरे प्राप्ते दशमे कन्यका बुधैः।

प्रदातव्या प्रयत्नेन न दोषः कालदोषतः ।"

"Damsels of eight, nine and ten years are respectively "named Gauri, Rohini, and Kanya; and all girls above ten "are called Rajaswala or women in their catamenia: when "therefore a girl has reached her tenth year, she is to be "immediately disposed of in marriage, and such marriage, "even though celebrated in an interdicted nuptial season, "will not be held culpable."

It thus appears, that Angira has fixed the eighth, ninth and tenth years as the proper marriageable age of a girl; and so great is his apprehension, lest she should continue unmarried after her tenth year, that he enjoins the marriage of a decennarian damsel even in times when weddings are forbidden; but with respect to males, he assigns neither twenty-four nor thirty years, nor any period for their marriageable age. Now it should be observed, whether or not, the above Texts of Manu and Angira contradict each other: Manu fixes either the eighth or twelfth year as the marriageable age of a girl, any deviation from which is declared by him to be sinful; while Angira directs that a damsel should be married in her eighth, ninth or tenth year, the last of which is declared to be the farthest limit, at which her marriage is indispensable and not to be deferred: hence, according to his opinion the twelfth year is by no means the proper marriageable age. The actual practice now-a-days is founded on the ordinance of Angira and opposed to the law of Manu. If the injunc-

* Quoted in the Udvahatattwa.

tion of Manu in this respect were to be followed, girls of eight and twelve years would be bestowed upon suitors aged twenty-four and thirty years respectivley; otherwise the sacred law is violated. We nowhere see, in the present age, the operation of such a rule. The ordinance of Angira, on the contrary, that the eighth, ninth, and tenth years are the proper wedding periods of a damsel, is almost universally observed. Hence then, as regards the determination of the marriageble age, the rule of Manu is at present discountenanced, while that of Angira, which is opposed to it, is respected.

Again, Manu has declared—

एक एवौरसः पुत्रः पित्र्यस्य वसुनः प्रभुः ।
शेषाणामानृशंस्यार्थं प्रदद्यात्तु प्रजीवनम् ॥ 9. 163.
षष्ठन्तु क्षेत्रजस्यांशं प्रदद्यात् पैतृकाद्धनात् ।
औरसो विभजन् दायं पित्र्यं पञ्चममेव वा ॥ 9. 164.
औरसक्षेत्रजौ पुत्रौ पितृरिक्थस्य भागिनौ ।
दशापरे तु क्रमशो गोत्ररिक्थांशभागिनः ॥ 9. 165.

"The son of his own body is the sole heir to a man's "estate. He is to allow a maintenance to the rest, out of "kindness only."

"But when the son of the body divides the paternal "inheritance, he is to give a sixth or fifth part of it to the "son of the wife begotten by a kinsman."

"The son of the body, and son of the wife should succeed to "the paternal estate, but the ten other kinds of sons succeed, "in order, to the family duties and to their share of inheritance."

Thus, according to Manu, if a man have many kinds of sons, a son of the body, a son of the wife, an adopted son and the like, then the son of the body shall inherit his paternal property, after having allotted to the son of the wife a fifth or sixth part of it ; and shall allow a maintenance to the adopted and other sons as a mere act of kindness ; on failure of a son of the body, the son of the wife shall succeed to the whole property, and failing him, the adopted son and so on ; the last named succeeding in default of the preceding.

But Katyayana says—

उत्पन्ने त्वौरसे पुत्रे तृतीयांशहराः सुताः ।
सवर्णा असवर्णास्तु ग्रासाच्छादनभागिनः ॥*

"On the birth of a son of the body, the other sons, of "the same caste with the father, take a third of his heritage ; "but if they be of a different caste, they are entitled only to "maintenance."

According to Katyayana, therefore, the son of the wife, the adopted and other sons, of the same caste with the father, succeed to a third of their paternal estate, and if of a different caste, can claim a mere maintenance. Mark now, whether or not Manu and Katyayana, are at variance with each other. Manu allows a sixth or a fifth of the heritage to the son of the wife and mere main-

* Quoted in the Dayabhaga.

tenance to the other kinds of sons; while Katyayana enjoins the allotment of a third part of the estate to the son of the wife as well as to all the rest, who are of the same class with the father. According to Manu, when there is a son of the body, the Dattaka (adopted son) is entitled only to maintenance; * but according to Katyayana, he has a claim to a third of the heritage. If we observe the actual practice, we shall find, that in this case, the injunction of Manu is disregarded, while that of Katyayana, who holds a contrary opinion, is followed: that is, in the present age when a son of the body is living, an adopted son, instead of getting mere maintenance, partakes of a third of the heritage. Had Vrihaspati meant to say that all Smritis, opposed to Manu, are to be rejected even in the Kali-yuga, how comes it that Katyayana's rule, in the case above cited, is now held valid in practice?

A third instance:

Manu says—

यस्या म्रियेत कन्याया वाचा सत्ये कृते पतिः ।
तामनेन विधानेन निजो विन्देत देवरः ॥ 9. 69.

* But if the Dattaka be endued with excellent qualities, he inherits the property with the son of the body. Thus:—

उपपन्नो गुणैः सर्वैः पुत्रो यस्य तु दत्त्रिमः ।
स हरेतैव तद्रिक्थं सम्प्राप्तोऽप्यन्यगोत्रतः ॥ 9. 141,

"Of the man, who has adopted a son adorned with every virtue, that son shall take the heritage though brought from a different family."

यथाविध्यधिगम्यैनां शुक्लवस्त्रां शुचिव्रताम् ।
मिथो भजेताप्रसवात् सकृत् सकृदृतावृतौ ॥ 9. 70.
न दत्त्वा कस्यचित् कन्यां पुनर्दद्याद्विचक्षणः ।
दत्त्वा पुनः प्रयच्छन् हि प्राप्नोति पुरुषानृतम् ॥ 9. 71.

"The damsel, whose husband dies after troth verbally "plighted but before consummation, his brother shall take "for the purpose of begetting a son on her according to this "rule."

"Having taken such a girl for the above purpose in due "form of law, she being clad in a white robe and pure in "her moral conduct, let him approach her once in due sea-"son, and until issue be had."

"Let no sensible man, who has once given his daughter to "a suitor, give her again (in the event of his death before "consummation) to another; for he who gives away his "daughter, whom he had before given, incurs the guilt of "stealing a girl."

We thus find that Manu prohibits the marriage of a betrothed girl on the death of the suitor to whom she had been plighted, directs the procreation of a son on her by his brother in due form of law, and, after the birth of such issue, enjoins the life-long observance of the rules of widowhood. According to his opinion, therefore, a betrothed girl is unmarriageable after the death of her suitor, and, for the perpetuation of his line, she, having, by his brother, given birth to a son, must continue a widow through her whole life.

But Vasishtha pronounces—

अद्भिर्वाचा च दत्तायां म्रियेताथो वरो यदि ।
न च मन्त्रोपनीता स्यात् कुमारी पितुरेव सा ॥
यावच्चेदाहृता कन्या मन्त्रैर्यदि न संस्कृता ।
अन्यस्मै विधिवद्देया यथा कन्या तथैव सा ॥ Ch. 17.

"The damsel, whose suitor happens to die after she had "been given to him by the sprinkling of water, or by troth "verbally plighted, but before the utterance of the nuptial "Texts, continues her father's."

"If a damsel has been given only by pledge of words "without the consummation of the marital act by the utter- "ance of the nuptial Texts, she should be bestowed upon "another in due form ; her state of celibacy is not des- "troyed by a mere verbal plight."

Thus Vasishtha, considering the virgin state of a betrothed girl unaffected by the death of the suitor before consummation, enjoins the bestowal of her to another in due form of law.

Observe now whether or not there is a broad contradiction between Manu and Vasishtha. Manu prohibits the marriage of a betrothed damsel after the death of the suitor before consummation, and directs her to bear a single son by her late suitor's brother, and then to continue a widow for life ; while Vasishtha plainly enjoins her wedding under the same predicament. On turning to the custom now prevailing in our country, we see it founded on the ordinance of Vasishtha ; that is, on the death of the suitor before consummation, a damsel is bestowed upon another according to the injunction of Vasishtha, but she is not, in conformity with the law of Manu, obliged to continue a widow for life.

When, therefore, on referring to practice we find, that in many particulars, Smritis opposed to Manu are every where respected and followed in the Kali-yuga, and when Parasara assigns the Dharmas propounded by Manu to be appropriate only to the Satya-yuga, the superiority of the authority of Manu, and the invalidity of Smritis opposed to him as declared by Vrihaspati, must necessarily be considered to allude to the Satya-yuga. Otherwise, the Text of Vrihaspati, that Manu has compiled the spirit of the Vedas, and therefore Manu is preeminent, becomes incongruous :—Has Manu alone digested in his Sanhita the purport of the Vedas, and have Yajnavalkya and Parasara and the other Rishis failed to do so? Have they, in their respective institutes, delivered their self-invented ordinances opposed to the Vodas? Certainly, it cannot be supposed that they knew not the Vedas, or that they did not propound, in their respective works, the spirit of the Vedas: the fact is, they have, in their respective Smritis, exhibited the scope of the Vedas in the same manner, as Manu has done in his own Sanhita.

If, then, what Vrihaspati has predicated of the institutes of Manu with a view to the establishment of his preeminence, can be equally predicated of the other institutes, how can the conclusion be rational that Manu is the supreme authority and the other Smriti writers are inferior to him. The same cause, which operates to render one work preeminent, must, while it exists in another, serve to render it equally excellent. In fact, when people regard all the Rishis equally wise and infallible, and when all of them have, in their respective works, propounded the spirit of the Vedas, all of them must, no doubt, be equally esteemed.

That we are to accord equal respect to all the Rishis is a conclusion arrived at not by myself alone ; Madhavacharya, in his commentary on the Parasara Sanhita, comes to the same decision.

Thus—

अस्तु वा यथाकथञ्चिन्मनुस्मृतेः प्रामाण्यं तथापि प्रकृतायाः पराशरस्मृतेः किमायातं तेन न हि मनोरिव पराशरस्य महिमानं कश्चिद्वेदः प्रख्यापयति तस्मात्तदीयस्मृतेर्दुर्निरूपं प्रामाण्यम्।

" Well ; if the preeminence of the institutes of Manu be, " in some such manner, established, what does it matter " with reference to the Parasara Sanhita ? Nowhere the " Vedas chant the greatness of Parasara as of Manu. It " would therefore be difficult to determine the authoritative- " ness of the institutes of Parasara."

Madhavacharya, having proposed this question, proceeds to solve it :

Thus—

नच पराशरमहिम्नोऽश्रौतत्वं [illegible] व्यासः पाराशर्य्य इति श्रुतौ पराशरपुत्रत्वमुपजीव्य व्यासस्य ख्यातत्वात्। यदा सर्व्वकर्मनियमनमहिम्नो वेदव्यासस्यापि ख्यातये पराशरपुत्रत्वमुप-

श्रीयते तदा किन्तु वक्तव्यमपि व्यासजनकतया पराशर इति । तस्मात् पराशरोऽपि मनुसमान एव । एष एव न्यायो वसिष्ठात्रियाज्ञवल्क्यादिषु बोद्धव्यः ।

"It is not true that Parasara's greatness has not "been chanted in the Vedas; by the expression in the "Vedas "Vyasa, the son of Parasara, has said" Vyasa "has been extolled as the son of Parasara. The eminence "of Vyasa is universally admitted; when, therefore, he has "been complimented in the Vedas for his being the son of "Parasara, it needs no mention, that Parasara's greatness "is beyond all question. Now, there remains no doubt, "that Parasara is, equally illustrious with Manu. Similar "reasoning should be applied to Vasishtha, Atri, Yajna-"valkya and others; that is, their greatness also being "sung in the Vedas, they are as exalted as Manu."

It is therefore indubitably established, that when all the sage authors of the Sanhitas are acknowledged to be equally wise and infallible; when all of them have, in their respective works, given an exposition of the spirit of the Vedas; and when they are all eulogized in the Vedas; all of them ought to receive from us an equal tribute of respect. The only distinction consists in this, that one special Text of Smriti obtains precedence in a particular Yuga: the institutes of Manu was the paramount authority in the Satya-yuga, those of Gotama in the Treta, those of Sankha and Likhita in the Dwapara, and those of Parasara is the cardinal Smriti in the Kali-yuga. Thus, the Smritis of Manu and Parasara being appropriate to two different Yugas, there is no such relation between them that any contradiction could be possible.

From all that have been urged above, we come to the following conclusions—

The institutes of Manu and Parasara, being the leading Sastras of two different Yugas, can never be at variance with each other; the superiority of Manu and the invalidity of Smritis opposed to him, as advanced by Vrihaspati, refer to the Satya-yuga; in the Kali-yuga, the Smritis, which are even at variance with Manu, are received as authorities. Hence, there can be no objection to the validity of the marriage of widows in the Kali-yuga as ordained by Parasara, even though it were opposed to the institutes of Manu.

Let us now inquire whether the nuptial ordinance of Parasara, in respect of widows and other women, is at all at variance with Manu or other Smritis.

Manu says—

या पत्या वा परित्यक्ता विधवा वा स्वयेच्छया।
उत्पादयेत् पुनर्भूत्वा स पौनर्भव उच्यते॥ 9. 175.

"If a woman, after becoming a widow, or being divorced
"by her husband, marries again, the son born of her of this
"marriage is called a Paunarbhava.

Vishnu says—

अक्षता भूयः संस्कृता पुनर्भूः। Ch. 15.

"She, who continues a virgin and undergoes the ceremony "of marriage for a second time, is called a Punarbhu."

Yajnavalkya declares—

अक्षता च क्षता चैव पुनर्भूः संस्कृता पुनः । 1. 67.

"She, who continues a virgin or otherwise, is called a Punarbhu, if she undergoes the ceremony of marriage for a second time."

Vasishtha pronounces—

या च क्लीबं पतितमुन्मत्तं वा पतिमुत्सृज्य अन्यं पतिं विन्दते मृते वा सा पुनर्भूर्भवति । Ch. 17.

"She, who having forsaken her lord for his impotence, "degradation, or insanity, or on his death, takes another hus-"band, is called a Punarbhu."

Thus, it appears, that Manu, Vishnu, Yajnavalkya, and Vasishtha, have admitted the remarriage of a woman, on the degradation, impotence, insanity, or the death, of her husband.

Some of the oppositionists have asserted that Manu and other Lawgivers, in making mention of the Paunarbhava (son born in the second wedlock of women), did not mean to legalize them, but only wanted to give a designation to such sons, should they happen to be born. This assumption, however, is gratuitous. No authorities warrant such a conclusion. For, those authors, who have declared the law with respect to sons, have one and all, regarded the Paunarbhava as a legal son.

Manu, after having defined the son of the body and the rest of the twelve kinds of sons, concludes with saying,

क्षेत्रजादीन् सुतानेतानेकादश यथोदितान्।
पुत्रप्रतिनिधीनाहुः क्रियालोपान्मनीषिणः॥ 9. 80.

" These eleven kinds of sons, the son of the wife and the
" rest as enumerated, are allowed by Rishis to be substi-
" tutes, in order, for a son of the body, for the sake of
" preventing the failure of obsequies."

And,

श्रेयसः श्रेयसोऽभावे पापीयान् रिक्थमर्हति। 9. 185.

" On failure of the superior classes of sons, in succession,
" let the inferior in order take the heritage."

Yajnavalkya, also, after describing the son of the body and the other kinds of sons, says,

पिण्डदोऽंशहरश्चैषां पूर्वाभावे परः परः। 2. 102.

" Among these twelve kinds of sons, when there is a fail-
" ure of those named first, they, who are named next in
" order, become the heir and the offerer of the funeral
" cake."

Thus, when Manu and Yajnavalkya have declared the Paunarbhava to have a legal right to the heritage and to the performance of the Sraddha, the assertion of such son's being illegal should be utterly disregarded.

When, therefore, Manu, Yajnavalkya, Vishnu, and Vasishtha admit the remarriage of women under certain contingencies, the conclusion that the marriage of widows is against the opinion of Manu and other Smriti writers must be quite unfounded. It would seem that this conclusion has been advanced by persons, who have not thoroughly studied Manu and other Jurists. It would be uncharitable to suppose, that with a full knowledge of the subject they have brought forward such an unfounded and a false statement.

The fact is, that the marriage of widows is not contrary to the opinion of Manu and other Jurists. The only thing to be marked is, that they designated the remarried females Punarbhus, and the sons, born in such second wedlock, Paunarbhavas: while, according to Parasara, such females and such sons are not to bear those designations in the Kali-yuga. This much is the extent of the difference of opinion between Parasara and the other Smriti writers Had Parasara intended to continue those designations in the Kali-yuga, he would certainly have assigned the term Punarbhu to such females and reckoned the Paunarbhava in his enumeration of the several kinds of sons. That, in the Kali-Yuga, such females are not to be called punarbhus and such sons, instead of being designated Paunarbhavas, are to be reckoned sons of the body, is borne out by the prevailing practice. Mark, if after troth verbally plighted, the suitor happens to die, or the match is broken by some cause or other, before consummation of the marital rite, the marriage of the damsel takes place with another person. In the preceding ages, such females were called Punarbhus and their issues Paunarbhavas.

Thus—

सप्त पौनर्भवाः कन्या वर्ज्जनीयाः कुलाधमाः।
वाचा दत्ता मनोदत्ता कृतकौतुकमङ्गला।
उदकस्पर्शिता या च या च पाणिगृहीतिका।
अग्निं परिगता या च पुनर्भूप्रभवा च या।
इत्येताः काश्यपेनोक्ता दहन्ति कुलमग्निवत्॥

"Seven Punarbhu (remarried) damsels, who are the despised "of their families, are to be shunned; the Vagdatta, she who "has been plighted by word of troth; the Manodatta, she "whom one has disposed of in his mind; the Krita-kautuka-"mangala, she on whose hand the nuptial string has been "tied; the Udaka-sparsita, she who has been given away by "the sprinkling of water; the Panigrihita, she in respect "of whom the ceremony of taking the hand has been "performed; Agnim parigata, she in respect of whom the "marriage ceremonies have been completed; and the Punar-"bhu-prabhava, she who is born of a Punarbhu: these "seven kinds of damsels described by Kasyapa, when mar-"ried, consume like fire the family of their husbands."

Now a days the marriage of four kinds of Punarbhus, out of the seven enumerated above, namely the Vagdatta, the Manodatta, the Krita-kautuka-mangala, and the Punarbhu-prabhava has become current. Such females have no distinctive appellation, and are regarded, in all respects, equal to the wives married for the first time, though in former Yugas they were designated Punarbhus, and the sons born of them, instead of being called Paunarbhavas, are to all intents and purposes, considered the same as the sons of the body. They offer funeral cakes to their parents, succeed to their estate, and perform all other stated duties just like a son of the body ; never, even by mistake, are they called Paunarbhavas.

It should now be observed, that, as the marriage of four, out of the seven kinds of Punarbhus of bygone ages, is now current, and they are deemed as reputable as women married for the first time, bearing even no distinctive appellation, and their issues undistinguished from the Aurasa putra (son of the body) ; if the second wedding of the remaining three Punarbhus were to come in vogue, by parity of reasoning, there would be no bar to their being regarded in the same light as wives married for the first time, and their sons being acknowledged as Aurasa putras (sons of the body).

Hence, then, as Parasara accords to the Punarbhu of the former ages the same right which is assigned to a once married woman, and to the Paunarbhavas of the past Yugas the same claims which are inherent in the Aurasa putra (son of the body), and as the prevailing custom upholds this opinion as regards the four kinds of Punarbhus and Paunarbhavas of the prior Yugas, there can be no doubt that remarried widows and their issue, though they might have been named Punarbhus and Paunarbhavas in the former Yugas, would now, in the Kali-yuga, be undistinguished from the first married wives and Aurasa putras (sons of the body) respectively.

The conclusion that sons of remarried widows are to

be regarded as Aurasa putras (sons of the body) in the Kali-yuga, is also fully supported by the authority of the Mahabharata wherein it is related, that there was a king of the Nagas, named Airavata, who married his widowed daughter to Arjuna, and the son born unto her by Arjuna, named Iravan, was reckoned as the Aurasa putra (son of the body) of Arjuna.

अर्जुनस्यात्मजः श्रीमानिरावान्नाम वीर्यवान् ।
सुतायां नागराजस्य जातः पार्थेन धीमता ॥
ऐरावतेन सा दत्ता ह्यनपत्या महात्मना ।
पत्यौ हते सुपर्णेन कृपणा दीनचेतना ॥*

" By Arjuna was begotten on the daughter of the king of " the Naga's a handsome and powerful son named Iravan: " when her husband was killed by Suparna, Airavata, the " magnanimous king of the Nagas, gave that dejected sorrow- " stricken childless daughter in marriage to Arjuna, the " third Pandava."

अजानन्नर्जुनश्चापि निहतं पुत्रमौरसम् ।
जघान समरे शूरान् राज्ञस्तान् भीष्मरक्षिणः ॥

" Arjuna, not knowing this his Aurasa putra (son of the " body) to have been killed, continued smiting the mighty " kings who defended Bhishma."

Thus it appears that with the setting in of the

* Bhishma Parva. Ch. 91.

Kali-yuga, * the Paunarbhava of the former Yugas, began to be reckoned and accepted as Aurasa putra (the son of the body).

We should now examine the spirit and real import of the Texts quoted by the oppositionists from Manu with the view of shewing that his opinion is adverse to the marriage of widows. The following half of one of the Texts of Manu has been cited by them to gain their object.

न द्वितीयश्च साध्वीनां क्वचिद्भर्त्तोपदिश्यते । 5. 162.

" And a stranger has not, in respect of a virtuous woman, " been ever called her husband in any Sastras."

But when its meaning and the purport of the context is considered, my adversaries will fail to attain their end.

Thus—

मृते भर्त्तरि साध्वी स्त्री ब्रह्मचर्य्ये व्यवस्थिता ।
स्वर्गं गच्छत्यपुत्रापि यथा ते ब्रह्मचारिणः ॥ 5. 160.
अपत्यलोभाद्या तु स्त्री भर्त्तारमतिवर्त्तते ।
सेह निन्दामवाप्नोति पतिलोकाच्च हीयते ॥ 5. 161.
नान्योत्पन्ना प्रजास्तीह न चाप्यन्यपरिग्रहे ।
न द्वितीयश्च साध्वीनां क्वचिद्भर्त्तोपदिश्यते ॥ 5. 162.

" That virtuous woman, who after the decease of her hus-

* शतेषु षट्सु सार्द्धेषु त्र्यधिकेषु च भूतले ।
कलेर्गतेषु वर्षाणामभवन् कुरुपाण्डवाः ॥

Six hundred and fifty three years after the Kali-yuga had commenced, the Kurus and Pandavas flourished.—Rajatarangini by Kalhana, Taranga I.

" band, observes the Brahmacharya, ascends to heaven though " she have no child ; like those Brahmacharis (abstemious " men) who had no issue."

" That woman, who from a wish to bear children prostitutes " herself, incurs opprobrium, and shall be excluded from the " seat of her husband (in another world)."

" Issue begotten on a woman by a stanger, is no progeny " of hers, and the child begotten on the wife of another man " is no offspring of the begetter ; and a stranger has not, " in respect of a virtuous woman, been ever called her hus- " band in any Sastras."

Vasishtha says—

अनन्ताः पुत्रिणां लोकाः नापुत्रस्य लोकोऽस्तीति श्रूयते। Ch. 17.

" Men having sons enjoy heaven to eternity ; it is declared " in theVedas, that heaven is not decreed for him, who has no " son."

If a childless widow, keeping this authority in view, fears her exclusion from heaven and, longing to gain it, receives the embraces of a stranger with the view of bearing a son, she brings disgrace upon herself and finds no place in heaven ; for issue illegally begotten by a stranger, is not to be reckoned her rightful child. If it be questioned, why not regard the begetter as her husband, Manu answers, no, " such a stranger has not, in respect of a virtuous woman, been ever called her husband in any Sastras ; that is, he, whom a woman, solely guided by her will, and in the hope of heaven, illegally betakes herself to, with the view of having a son procreated on her, can, according to no Sastras, be regarded her husband. Since, all the Sastras have applied the term husband to that man only, with whom a woman has been married in due form established by law.

The proper import, therefore, of half the Text, quoted by the replicants, is, that if a widow, yearning for a son in the hope of heaven, *prostitutes* herself by receiving the embraces of a stranger, that stranger cannot be called her *husband;* otherwise, if it imply, that a woman can have no *second husband* even though she *marry* him in due legal form, it would jar with the injunction of Manu himself in respect of the Paunarbhavas, whom he allows to offer funeral cakes to their parents and succeed to their property.

The replicants have made a second attempt to establish the discordance of the marriage of widows with Manu, by accepting an absolutely verbal import of another half of a Text of Manu, without examining its bearing with the context.

Thus—

न विवाहविधावुक्तं विधवावेदनं पुनः ।

" In the nuptial ordinances there is no mention of the " remarriage of widows."

But they have failed to see that if this Text were to be considered positively prohibitory of the marriage of widows, it would be at variance with Manu's own legalization of Paunarbhava. The half of the Text, cited above, taken by itself, may some how be construed in the spirit in which they have interpreted it; but when viewed in its relation with the context and the end and scope of the author, this interpretation can never be maintained.

Thus—

देवराद्वा सपिण्डाद्वा स्त्रिया सम्यङ्नियुक्तया ।
प्रजेप्सिताधिगन्तव्या सन्तानस्य परिक्षये ॥ 9. 59.
विधवायां नियुक्तस्तु घृताक्तो वाग्यतो निशि ।
एकमुत्पादयेत् पुत्रं न द्वितीयं कथञ्चन ॥ 9. 60.
द्वितीयमेके प्रजनं मन्यन्ते स्त्रीषु तद्विदः ।
अनिर्वृत्तं नियोगार्थं पश्यन्तो धर्मतस्तयोः ॥ 9. 61.
विधवायां नियोगार्थे निर्वृत्ते तु यथाविधि ।
गुरुवच्च स्नुषावच्च वर्तेयातां परस्परम् ॥ 9. 62.
नियुक्तौ यौ विधिं हित्वा वर्तेयातां तु कामतः ।
तावुभौ पतितौ स्यातां स्नुषागगुरुतल्पगौ ॥ 9. 63.
नान्यस्मिन् विधवा नारी नियोक्तव्या द्विजातिभिः ।
अन्यस्मिन् हि नियुञ्जाना धर्मं हन्युः सनातनम् ॥ 9. 64.
नोद्वाहिकेषु मन्त्रेषु नियोगः कीर्त्यते क्वचित् ।
न विवाहविधावुक्तं विधवावेदनं पुनः ॥ 9. 65.
अयं द्विजैर्हि विद्वद्भिः पशुधर्मो विगर्हितः ।
मनुष्याणामपि प्रोक्तो वेने राज्यं प्रशासति ॥ 9. 66.
स महीमखिलां भुञ्जन् राजर्षिप्रवरः पुरा ।
वर्णानां सङ्करं चक्रे कामोपहतचेतनः ॥ 9. 67.
ततः प्रभृति यो मोहात् प्रमीतपतिकां स्त्रियम् ।
नियोजयत्यपत्यार्थं तं विगर्हन्ति साधवः ॥ 9. 68.

"On failure of issue, a wife, duly authorised, may have "the desired son begotten on her by the husband's brother or "by some other kinsman."

"Sprinkled with clarified butter and silent, in the night, "let the man thus appointed beget one son, but a second by "no means, on that widow."

"Some sages, versed in the rules of appointment, thinking "that the legal object of the appointmet may not be answered, "by the birth of a single son, enjoin the procreation of a "second son on the widow."

"The object of the appointment having, in respect of the "widow, been legally accomplished, they both (the widow "and the man appointed) are to live like a daughter-in-law "and a father-in-law."

"They two, who being appointed for the above purpose, "deviate from the strict rule and act from carnal desire, "shall be degraded and deemed the one as having defiled the "bed of his daughter-in-law, and the other as having "criminally lived with her father-in-law."

"By men of twice born classes no widow must be autho-"rized to conceive by a stranger ; by such an authorization "to conceive by a stranger, chastity is ruined."

"Nowhere in the nuptial Texts, has Niyoga (appointment) "been mentioned, and in marital ordinances, the Vedana "(acceptance for the purpose of procreating) of a widow is "not alluded to."

"This practice, fit only for cattle, is reprehended by the "learned twice-born ; it is said to have been the custom "even amongst men, while Vena had sovereign power."

"That great monarch, having grasped the whole earth, "and having lost sense through lust, gave rise to the Var-"na-sankara (mixed classes)."

"Since that time, the virtuous condemn that man who, "through delusion of mind, appoints a widow to have a son "procreated on her."

Now, on duly considering these Texts, would it appear that they treat of the marriage of widows or of Kshetraja putras (sons born on the wife by another) ? The first Text introduces and the last concludes the subject of Kshetraja putra. When, therefore, the proem and the sequel relate to injunctions and prohibitions respecting the kshetraja putra and all the intermediate Texts allude to the same subject, there can be no doubt that this section treats of the procreation of a son on another's wife. As regards the Text (included in the above cited ones), on the strength of which the oppositionists urge that the marriage of widows is against the opinion of Manu, I have to say that, as in the first half of it the word Niyoga has been used, which clearly and indisputably signifies direction for the procreation of a son on another's wife, the ambiguous term Vedana in the second half must also be taken, regard being had to the context, in the sense of acceptance of another's wife for the procreation of a son. The verbal radix Vid (to accept), from which the word Vedana is derived, means *to accept* the hand of a woman, either in marriage or for the purpose of procreating on her a Kshetraja son ; Vedana, therefore, signifies marriage or taking for the above purpose, according as it is used in a passage relating to nuptial matters or to the practice of Niyoga or appointment.

Thus—

न सगोत्रां न समानप्रवरां भार्यां विन्देत ।*

* Vishnu Sanhita. Ch. XXIV.

"A damsel of the same kin *Na vindeta*, that is, one "should not take as a wife."

Here, the passage relates to nuptial matters, and the derivative Vindeta from the verb Vid necessarily signifies taking the hand in marriage.

Again—

यस्या म्रियेत कन्याया वाचा सत्ये कृते पतिः ।
तामनेन विधानेन निजो विन्देत देवरः ॥
यथाविध्यधिगम्यैनां शुक्लवस्त्रां शुचिव्रताम् ।
मिथो भजेताप्रसवात् सकृत् सकृदृतावृतौ ॥

"The damsel, whose suitor dies after troth verbally "plighted, but before consummation, his brother, according "to this rule, *Vindeta*, that is, shall take for the purpose of "begetting a son on her."

"Having taken in due form such a girl, bearing all the "marks of widowhood, for the above purpose, let him ap- "proach her once in due season and until issue be had."

Here the Texts obviously treat of Niyoga or direction for the procreation of a son on another's wife: hence, the verb Vid, through its derivative Vindeta, is accepted in the sense of taking for the procreation of a son &c. It is conclusive, therefore, that, in the following Text—

न विवाहविधावुक्तं विधवावेदनं पुनः ।

"In the matrimonial ordinances the Vedana of a woman "is not alluded to."

the word Vedana, derived from the verb Vid, being used in the passage relating to Niyoga, must necessarily mean acceptance for the procreation of a son; otherwise, all sense and consistency would be destroyed. The two interpretations of the Text in question are here placed in juxta position, to enable the reader to judge of their respective correctness and appositeness.

"Nowhere in the nuptial Mantras (specific Texts) has
" Niyoga (direction for the procreation of a son &c.) been
" mentioned, nor in the matrimonial ordinances *has the*
" *taking of a widow for the procreation of a son on her been*
" *alluded to.*"

"Nowhere in the nuptial Mantras (speific Texts) has
" Niyoga (direction for the procreation of a son &c.) been
" mentioned, nor in the matrimonial ordinances, *has the mar-*
" *riage of a widow been alluded to.*"

Manu, in this passage, wishes to interdict Niyoga Dharma (practice of appointment), and, therefore, distinctly prohibits it by saying that among all the Mantras (specific Texts) relating to marriage, there are none, which make mention of Niyoga, nor is there in the injunction relating to marriage any allusion to Vedana, (accepting of a woman for the purpose of procreating a child on her): that is, as Niyoga (direction for &c.) is a means for the generation of progeny, and as the great object of marriage is the begetting of a son, Manu reckons Niyoga and Vedana as a sort of marriage, and from the circumstance of their not being mentioned in the nuptial Mantras or marital ordinances, concludes Niyoga to be illegal. It is hard to conceive that having, in the first half of a Text in the section on Niyoga, prohibited the procreation of a Kshetraja son, he would, in the second half of it, introduce the irrelevant and impertinent prohibition of the marriage of widows, It is quite in keeping with the section on Niyoga to say, that the Niyoga Dharma is not mentioned in the nuptial mantras, but it does not accord with the spirit of that section to say, that the marriage of widows is not alluded to, in the marital ordinances. Why would the question of the marriage of widows be suddenly started, while the author is discussing the Niyoga Dharma? In fact, in the Text in question, the term Vedana has been used and not the term Vevaha (marriage). The Vedana has the double import of taking the hand in marriage and acceptance for the procreation of a child according to the Niyoga Dharma. Here it unquestionably means, from the context, accepting a woman for the procreation of a child on her. They, who attempt to make it here signify formal marriage and thereby to establish the prohibition of the marriage of widows, betray only their ignorance of the spirit of the passage.

That this section treats of Niyoga only, and not the marriage of widows, would be further corroborated by what Vrihaspati, the preceptor of the gods, has said in reference to these Texts of Manu.

Thus—

उक्तो नियोगो मनुना निषिद्धः स्वयमेव तु ।
युगह्रासादशक्योऽयं कर्तुमन्यैर्विधानतः ॥

तपोज्ञानसमायुक्ताः कृतत्रेतादिके नराः ।
द्वापरे च कलौ नृणां शक्तिहानिर्हि निर्मिता ॥
अनेकधा कृताः पुत्रा ऋषिभिर्ये पुरातनैः ।
न शक्यास्तेऽधुना कर्तुं शक्तिहीनैरिदन्तनैः ॥*

"Manu himself has enjoined Niyoga (direction for &c.) "and has himself interdicted it. Human power decreasing "according to the Yugas, people are not able strictly to "follow the Niyoga rules; men in the Satya, Treta, and "Dwapara Yugas were given to devotion and austerities and "blessed with higher intellectual powers, but in the Kali-"yuga, the human race has degenerated; the various kinds "of sons which were created by the sages of old, cannot now "be created by the weak mortals of the present age."

That is, in the section on Niyoga, Manu has, in the first five Texts, clearly ordained the Niyoga, while in the remaining five, he has as clearly interdicted it. It would be certainly absurd for the same person enjoining and prohibiting the same thing in the same breath. The auspicious Vrihaspati has solved this difficulty, by declaring that Manu intended to refer the injunction for Niyoga to the Satya, Treta, and Dwapara Yugas, and its prohibition to the Kali-yuga: hence it appears undeniable, from Vrihaspati's exposition of the section on Niyoga in the institutes of Manu, that it treats only of that subject.

It should also be observed here, that the institutes of Narada are a portion of the institutes of Manu, Narada

* Quoted by Kuiluka Bhatta.

having abridged the larger work of Manu, his compilation has been styled the Narada-Sanhita, just as the work, which now passes under the name of Manu Sanhita, is sometimes called the Bhrigu-Sanhita, because, it has been compiled by Bhrigu. We find in the beginning of the Narada Sanhita the following passage :

भगवान् मनुः प्रजापतिः सर्वभूतानुग्रहार्थमाचारस्थितिहेतुभूतं शास्त्रं चकार। तदेतत् श्लोकशतसहस्रमासीत्। तेनाध्यायसहस्रेण मनुः प्रजापतिरुपनिबध्य देवर्षये नारदाय प्रायच्छत्। स च तस्मादधीत्य महत्त्वाद्ग्रन्थस्य सुदुष्करो मनुष्याणां धारयितुमिति द्वादशभिः सहस्रैः संचिक्षेप तच्च सुमतये भार्गवाय प्रायच्छत्। स च तस्मादधीत्य तथैवायुर्ह्रासादल्पीयसी मनुष्याणां शक्तिरिति ज्ञात्वा चतुर्भिः सहस्रैः संचिक्षेप। तदेतत् सुमतिकृतं मनुष्या अधीयते। विस्तरेण शतसाहस्रं देवगन्धर्वादयः। यत्रायमाद्यः श्लोको भवति

आसीदिदं तमोभूतं न प्राज्ञायत किञ्चन।
ततः स्वयम्भूर्भगवान् प्रादुरासीच्चतुर्मुखः॥

इत्येवमधिकृत्य क्रमात् प्रकरणात् प्रकरणमनुक्रान्तम्। तत्र तु नवमं प्रकरणं व्यवहारो नाम यस्येमां देवर्षिर्नारदः सूत्रस्थानीयां मातृकां चकार।

"The auspicious Manu has prepared his Sastra as a means "for preserving the purity of the Acharas (practices) of mor- "tals. Manu having written that work in a hundred thou- "sand couplets, arranged in a thousand chapters, dilivered "the work to Narada, the divine sage, who studied it "under Manu himself, and thinking it difficult for men to be "edified in the Sastra, comprised in a work of so great a "magnitude, abridged it into twelve thousand verses, in "order to render it easy of acquisition. The Epitome he "gave to a descendant of Bhrigu, named Sumati, who having "received instructions in it from him, and observing the "decrease of human power owing to the diminution of the "period of human life, further reduced it into four thousand "verses. Mortals read only this abridgment by Sumati, "while Devas (gods) and gandharvas (heavenly choristers) "study the primary great work consisting of hundred thou-"sand verses, which commences with the following couplet. "'This universe was involved in darkness, nothing was per-"ceptible : then appeared the auspicious and quadruvisaged "Brahma the uncreated Being.' After this commencement, "the various sections follow each other in regular succession ; "among them the ninth is on the administration of justice ; "thus the divine Narada has introdoed the subject."

It is manifest, therefore, that the institutes of Narada are but the essence of the larger edition of the institutes of Manu, Narada having epitomized the great work of Manu, comprised in a hundred thousand couplets. Now, as has been shown elsewhere, that in Narada's abridgment of the institutes of Manu, there is an injunction for the remarriage of women under five predicaments, namely, when tidings are not received of a husband and the like, such an injunction is to be considered not only as delivered by Parasara but also by Manu himself; for this reason, in Madhavacharya's commentary on Parasara, the Text beginning with "On receiving no tidings of a husband &c." has been quoted as the Text of Manu."

Thus—

मनुरपि

नष्टे मृते प्रव्रजिते क्लीबे च पतिते पतौ ।
पञ्चस्वापत्सु नारीणां पतिरन्यो विधीयते ॥

"Manu also has said,

"On receiving no tidings of a husband, on his demise, on "his turning an ascetic, on his being found impotent, or on "his degradation, under any one of these five calamities, it "is canonical for women to take another husband."

We are thus warranted in concluding that the marriage of widows, instead of being opposed to, is perfectly in accordance with, the opinion of Manu, and when Parasara cites the above Text of Manu verbatim and literatim, it is a vain attempt to prove that the marriage of widows is against the law of Manu.

CHAPTER IV.

The Marital Text of Parasara is not opposed to the Vedas.

Some of the replicants have attempted to prove, that the injunction of Parasara for the remarriage of females is contrary to the spirit of the Vedas. Their object in so doing is, that as the Vedas are the paramount authority in this country the ordinance of Parasara, if opposed to them, cannot be accepted as a rule of conduct, inasmuch as it has been settled by Vedavyasa, that

श्रुतिस्मृतिपुराणानां विरोधो यत्र दृश्यते ।
तत्र श्रौतं प्रमाणन्तु तयोर्द्वैधे स्मृतिर्वरा ॥

"Where variance is observed between the Veda, the "Smriti, and the Purana, there the Veda is the supreme au-"thority: where the Smriti and Purana contradict each other "Smriti is the supreme authority."

The following is the Vaidic Text cited by the oppositionists:

यदेकस्मिन् यूपे द्वे रशने परिव्ययति तस्मादेको द्वे जाये विन्देत ।
यन्नैकां रशनां द्वयोर्यूपयोः परिव्ययति तस्मान्नैका द्वौ पती विन्देत ॥

"As round a single Yupa (sacrificial post) two tethers "can be tied, so a man can marry two wives. As one tether "cannot be tied round two Yupas, so a woman cannot marry "two husbands."

Their assumption, that the marriage of widows is an anti-vaidic doctrine, rests on this Text alone. My adversaries, on meeting with the passage "a woman cannot marry two husbands," have jumped to the conclusion that the marriage of widows is opposed to the Vedas. This is not, however, the real purport of this Text of the Vedas. The meaning of the above cited passage is, that as round a single Yupa two tethers can *at the same time* be fastened, so one man can *at the same time* have two wives; and as one tether cannot *at the same time* be tied round two Yupas, so one woman cannot *at the same time* have two husbands ; not that, on the death of the first husband, she cannot have a second. This interpretation is not merely the result of my individual cogitation ; it is corroborated by a Text of the Vedas themselves, quoted by Nilakantha, one of the Commentators of the Mahabharata, and by his exposition of that Text.

Text—

नैकस्या बहवः सह पतयः ।*

" A woman cannot have many husbands *together*."

Commentary—

सहेति युगपद्बहुपतित्वनिषेधो विहितो न तु क्रमभेदेन । †

" The word Saha (*together*) in this Vaidic Text means that " a woman is prohibited from having many husbands *at the* " *same time*, but her having many husbands *at different times* " is not reprehensible."

Thus, the attempt of my adversaries to prove the marriage of widows as opposed to the Vedas has failed. They ought to have considered that the Rishis, who are admitted to have compiled in their Sanhitas the spirit of the Vedas, would never have permitted such marriage, nor could the practice have prevailed in ancient times, had it been interdicted in the Vedas.

* This Text has also been quoted by Madhavacharya in his commentary on the Parasara Sanhita.

† Adi Parva, Ch. 195.

CHAPTER VIII.

Restrictions of Dirghatama are not prohibitory of the Marriage of Widows.

Some of the replicants have asserted upon the authority of the following Text, quoted from the Adi Parva of the Mahabharata, that a woman should have only one husband in this world:

दीर्घतमा उवाच ।

अद्यप्रभृति मर्य्यादा मया लोके प्रतिष्ठिता ।
एक एव पतिर्नार्य्या यावज्जीवं परायणम् ॥
मृते जीवति वा तस्मिन्नापरं प्राप्नुयान्नरम् ।
अभिगम्य परं नारी पतिष्यति न संशयः ॥

They have interpreted the Text thus—"Dirghatama says: that a woman shall adhere to *one* husband only during her life. Neither after his death nor during his lifetime, shall she have intercourse with another man. If she have such intercourse, she shall surely be degraded." If this interpretation were correct, their objection to the marriage of widows would certainly be valid. But the Text has a different signification altogether. It means that a woman should adhere to her husband *alone* as long as she lives; neither after his death nor during his lifetime, shall she have intercourse with another man &c. The passage appears to have reference to criminal connection which was prevalent in early ages, and not to marriage.

That adultery did prevail in early ages, is observed in another part of the Mahabharata.

Thus—

ऋतावृतौ राजपुत्रि स्त्रिया भर्त्ता पतिव्रते ।
नातिवर्त्तव्य इत्येवं धर्म्मं धर्म्मविदो विदुः ॥
शेषेष्वन्येषु कालेषु स्वातन्त्र्यं स्त्री किलार्हति ।
धर्म्ममेवं जनाः सन्तः पुराणं परिचक्षते ॥*

Pandu says to Kunti. "O Chaste Princess! persons learned "in religion admit it to be the religious duty of women not "to neglect their husbands during the menses: at other "times, women may gratify their own inclinations, and pious "men have sung of this ancient Dharma (practice)."

That is, during the menses, women, for the sake of the genuineness of the offspring, should attend their husbands only, and not have intercourse with other men; but at other times, they might live with other men. This practice was sanctioned in early ages by pious men. Dirghatama issues his injunction to put a stop to this long prevailing practice of women indulging themselves according to their inclinations, and his prohibition of intercourse with other men evidently refers to *adultery,* not to *second marriage* contracted agreeably to the Sastras. The same will appear from the context:

पुत्रलाभाच्च सा पत्नी न तुतोष पतिं तदा ।
प्रद्विषन्तीं पतिर्भार्यां किं मां द्वेक्षीति चाब्रवीत् ॥

* Mahabharata. Adi Parva. Ch. 122.

प्रद्वेष्युवाच ।

भार्य्याया भरणाद्भर्ता पालनाच्च पतिः स्मृतः ।
अहं त्वां भरणं कृत्वा जात्यन्धं ससुतं सदा ।
नित्यकालं श्रमेणार्त्ता न भरेयं महातपः ॥
तस्यास्तद्वचनं श्रुत्वा ऋषिः कोपसमन्वितः ।
प्रत्युवाच ततः पत्नीं प्रद्वेषीं ससुतां तदा ।
नीयतां क्षत्रियकुलं धनार्थश्च भविष्यति ॥

प्रद्वेष्युवाच ।

त्वया दत्तं धनं विप्र नेच्छेयं दुःखकारणम् ।
यथेष्टं कुरु विप्रेन्द्र न भरेयं यथा पुरा ॥

दीर्घतमा उवाच ।

अद्यप्रभृति मर्य्यादा मया लोके प्रतिष्ठिता ।
एक एव पतिर्नार्य्या यावज्जीवं परायणम् ॥
मृते जीवति वा तस्मिन्नापरं प्राप्नुयान्नरम् ।
अभिगम्य परं नारी पतिष्यति न संशयः ॥
अपतीनान्तु नारीणामद्यप्रभृति पातकम् ।
यद्यस्ति चेद्धनं सर्वं वृथाभोगा भवन्तु ताः ।
अकीर्त्तिः परिवादाश्च नित्यं तासां भवन्तु वै ॥
इति तद्वचनं श्रुत्वा ब्राह्मणी भृशकोपिता ।
गङ्गायां नीयतामेष पुत्रा इत्येवमब्रवीत् ॥
लोभमोहाभिभूतास्ते पुत्रास्तु गौतमादयः ।
बद्ध्वोडुपे परिक्षिप्य गङ्गायां समवासृजन् ॥
कस्मादन्धश्च वृद्धश्च भर्त्तव्योऽयमिति स्म ह ।
चिन्तयित्वा ततः क्रूराः प्रतिजग्मुरथो गृहान् ॥

" Dirghatama's wife, who had already offspring, no lou-
" ger gratifying him, Dirghatama asked her the reason why
" she slighted him. She replied 'a husband maintains his wife
" and is therefore called Bharta, (supporter). He takes care
" of her and is therefore called her Pati (lord); but you are
" born blind, and I have been always put to as much trouble
" as possible to support you and your children. I will do so
" no more.' Hearing this from his wife, the Rishi, full
" of anger, asked his wife and children to take him to the
" king whereby they would gain wealth. His wife rejoined : 'I
" do not want wealth acquired by you ; you can do what you
" like ; I will no longer maintain you.' Dirghatama said,
" 'from this day I ordain, for this world, that a woman shall
" adhere to her husband alone as long as she lives. Neither
" after his death nor during his lifetime, shall she have in-
" tercourse with another man. She who does so shall be
" surely degraded. From this day, women, neglecting their
" husbands and having intercourse with other men, shall be
" sinful, shall not be able to enjoy riches if they are posses-
" ed of any, and shall always be infamous.' Dirghatama's
" wife, hearing this, asked her sons to throw him into the
" Ganges. Gotama and other sons, blinded by avarice, and
" thinking it useless to support a blind and an old father,
" tied him to a float and left him floating on the river."

It is evident from the above, that Dirghatama resenting his wife's refusal to support him any longer, enjoined that a woman shall adhere to her husband alone, and that women neglecting their husbands shall be sinful. Seeing himself slighted by his wife, he imagined she was thinking of abandoning him, to have intercourse with another man ; and being wrathful at this, he issued his injunction to put a stop to the long prevailing practice of women indulging themselves according to their inclinations. This practice was regarded as a Dharma by pious men in early ages, and they imputed no guilt to it. Consequently, Dirghatama's wife would not have been culpable or sinful by adopting it ; and hence Dirghatama ordained, that a woman committing adultery shall be degraded and culpable. If Dirghtama's injunction be interpreted to imply that a woman shall not have intercourse with another man or marry him under any circumstances, even in accordance to the injunctions of Sastras, how could Dirghatama himself immediately after procreate a Kshetraja son on Sudeshna the queen of King Vali.

सोऽनुस्रोतस्तदा विप्रः प्लवमानो यदृच्छया।
जगाम सुबहून् देशानन्धस्तेनोडुपेन ह॥
तन्तु राजा बलिर्नाम सर्व्वधर्म्मविदां वरः।
अपश्यन्मज्जनगतः स्रोतसाभ्याशमागतम्॥
जग्राह चैनं धर्म्मात्मा बलिः सत्यपराक्रमः।
ज्ञात्वैनं स च वव्रेऽथ पुत्रार्थे भरतर्षभ॥
सन्तानार्थं महाभाग भार्य्यासु मम मानद।
पुत्रान् धर्म्मार्थकुशलानुत्पादयितुमर्हसि॥
एवमुक्तः स तेजस्वी तं तथेत्युक्तवानृषिः।
तस्मै स राजा स्वां भार्य्यां सुदेष्णां प्राहिणोत्तदा॥

"The blind Brahmana, floating at random in the stream, "passed through many countries. King Vali, superior to all "in the knowledge of religion, was bathing in the Ganges, "when he saw the old Brahmana floating close to him on

"the stream. The king immediately seized him, and learn-
"ing all the particulars, requested him to procreate a vir-
"tuous and able son on his queen. Dirghatama accepted the
"offer, and the king sent Sudeshna to him."

Hence, if Dirghatama's injunction had condemned as sinful a woman's intercourse with another man than the husband, even according to the rules prescribed by the Sastras, he himself would not have agreed to violate his own injunction, by undertaking to procreate a son on the queen of king Vali. He would have certainly prevented the king from giving his queen to another man for the procreation of a son. Again, in another part of the Mahabharata, it will be found that Arjuna married the widowed daughter of the Naga-raja Airavata. If Dirghatama's injunction had been prohibitory of the marriage of widows, then Naga-raja Airavata, after the issuing of the injunction, would not have offered his widowed daughter in marriage, and Arjuna also would not have married the widow. In fact, the procreation of sons by another man, and remarriage after the death of the husband, are consonant to the Sastras; and Dirghatama's condemnation of the long prevailing practice of adultery, not sanctioned by Sastras, cannot interfere with these. Hence, it is evident that Dirghatama has prescribed his rule only to prohibit the long existing evil practice of adultery

Let us examine the passage in another way. Even admitting that it has reference to the remarriage of women, it cannot by any means be said to support the oppositionists in their assertion that the injunction of Dirghatama is prohibitory of such marriage. For, as the Text does not mention any particular Yuga, it is to be considered as a general rule applicable to all the Yugas. The Text of Parasara applies, as has already been stated, to the Kali-yuga only, and is therefore a special rule on the subject. As in cases where there are both general and special rules, the latter always supercede the former, so in the present instance, Parasara's rule must supercede that of Dirghatama. Should Dirghatama's rule be admitted to apply to the Kali-yuga only, even then, it cannot be understood to prohibit the remarriage of women altogether. For, this rule enjoins general prohibition, while Parasara makes five exceptions in which remarriage is allowable. The special rule must supercede the general one.

CHAPTER X.

The Parasara Sanhita teaches the Dharmas of the Kali-yuga alone and not of other Yugas.

Some have raised an objection, that it is not only the Dharmas of the Kali-yuga that have been set down in the Parasara Sanhita, but the Dharmas of the other

Yugas have been set down also. The purport of this objection seems to be, that if it is proved that the Dharmas of the other Yugas, besides those of the Kali, had been declared in the Parasara Sanhita, then the rule, which Parasara has laid down for the marriage of widows and other wedded women, would apply to those Yugas and not to Kali ; and thus the marriage of widows would not be consonant to the Sastras in the Kali-yuga. In the Parasara Sanhita, the sacrifice of the horse ; the eating of the rice of a Dasa, Napita, Gopala, and some others of the Sudra caste ; the shortening of the period of Asaucha (impurity) of a twice-born in case he is a student of the Vedas &c. are enjoined. The opponents, supposing these to be the Dharmas of Satya, Treta, and Dwapara, and not of Kali, have raised the objection under review. But, from what has been proved before, it is clear that the sole object of the Parasara Sanhita is to enjoin the Dharmas of the Kali-yuga alone. So, there is not a shade of plausibility to suppose, that the Dharmas of the other Yugas should be enjoined in that Sanhita. The sacrifice of horse &c., therefore, from the purport and aim of the Sanhita, cannot be proved to be the Dharmas of the other Yugas alone. The opponents, finding in the Adi, Vrihannaradiya and Aditya Puranas the sacrifice of the horse &c. interdicted in the Kali-yuga, have concluded them to be the Dharmas of the other Yugas. The line of argument they seem to have adopted in their minds is this: "In the preceding Yugas the sacrifice of the horse &c. were permitted and performed. But it is found that in some

Sastras they are prohibited in the Kali-yuga. They, therefore, cannot be the Dharmas of that Yuga. Hence, when they are enjoined in the Parasara Sanhita, it is evident that in that Sanhita the Dharmas of the Yugas other than the Kali are set down also."

In order to meet this objection, we should see, in the first instance, whether the interdiction of the Adi, Vrihannaradiya, and Aditya Puranas have, all along in the Kali-yuga, been observed as such. We have no history of the manners and customs of our country. Complete success, therefore, in the inquiry is impossible. But, from as much as can be learned by a careful investigation, it is clearly demonstrated that the interdiction of the Puranas, mentioned above, has not been observed as such. We have distinct evidence of some of those Dharmas having been performed in the Kali-yuga which are interdicted in those three works. When, therefore, in the face of the interdiction, those Dharmas have been performed, how can it be maintained that the interdiction has been properly observed as such? The marriage of a wedded woman; the allotment of the best share to the eldest brother; sea-voyage; turning an ascetic; the marriage of the twice born men with damsels not of the same caste; procreation on a brother's widow or wife; the slaughter of cattle in the entertainment of a guest; repast on flesh meat at sacrifices for the satisfaction of departed ancestors; entrance into the order of Vanaprastha (hermit); the giving of a damsel to a bridegroom a second time, after she has been given to another; Brahmacharya continued for a long time; the sacrifice of a man, horse, or bull; walking on a pilgrimage till the pilgrim die; entrance into fire; the rule of expiation for Brahmanas extending to death; the filiation of no other sons than the Dattaka (son given) and Aurasa (son by birth); the diminution of the period of Asaucha, (impurity) in proportion to the purity of character and the extent of erudition in the Vedas; the eating of edibles offered by a Dasa, Napita, Gopala &c. of the Sudra caste; these Dharmas and some others are stated in the Adi, Vrihannaradiya and Aditya Puranas as those, the observance of which is interdicted in the Kali-yuga. Of these, the sacrifice of horse, entrance into fire, turning an ascetic, Bramacharya for a long time, sea-voyage, distant pilgrimage and the marriage of widows are the Dharmas, of the observance of which in the Kali-yuga we have clear evidence.

Thus:—

The Pandavas, who flourished 653 years after the Kali-yuga had commenced, performed the sacrifice of horse and went on a distant pilgrimage. These are facts so well and universally known, that to adduce proofs thereof is superfluous. It has also been stated before (P. 76.) that Arjuna married the widowed daughter of the Naga-raja Airavata.

A king of the name of Sudraka flourished a few centuries before the birth of Vikramaditya. We have clear evidence of his having performed the sacrifice of horse and of entering fire.

Thus :—

ऋग्वेदं सामवेदं गणितमथ कलां वैशिकीं हस्तिशिक्षां
ज्ञात्वा शर्वप्रसादाद्व्यपगततिमिरे चक्षुषी चोपलभ्य ।
राजानं वीक्ष्य पुत्रं परमसमुदयेनाश्वमेधेन चेष्ट्वा
लब्ध्वा चायुः शताब्दं दशदिनसहितं शूद्रकोऽग्निं प्रविष्टः ॥ *

" He (Sudraka) was well versed in the Rik and Sama Vedas, " in the Mathematical Science, in the sixty-four elegant arts, " and the management of elephants : by the favor of Siva " he enjoyed eyes uninvaded by darkness, and beheld his " son seated on the throne : after performing the exalted " Aswamedha (the sacrifice of horse) and having attained the " age of an hundred years and ten days, he entered the " fatal fire." †

* Mrichchhakati. Prelude.

† In the chapter of prophecies in the Skanda Purana we find a mention of this Sudraka.

Thus :—

त्रिषु वर्षसहस्रेषु कलेर्यातेषु पार्थिव ।
त्रिशते च दशन्यूने ह्यस्यां भुवि भविष्यति ।
शूद्रको नाम वीराणामधिपः सिद्धसत्तमः ॥
नृपान् सर्वान् पापरूपान् वर्द्धितान् यो हनिष्यति ।
चर्चितायां समाराध्य लप्स्यते भूभरापहः ॥
ततस्त्रिषु सहस्रेषु दशाधिकशतत्रये ।
भविष्यं नन्दराज्यञ्च चाणक्यो यान् हनिष्यति ।
शुक्लतीर्थे सर्वपापनिर्मुक्तिं योऽभिलप्स्यते ॥
ततस्त्रिषु सहस्रेषु सहस्राभ्यधिकेषु च ।
भविष्यो विक्रमादित्यो राज्यं सोऽत्र प्रलप्स्यते ॥

We have clear evidence of a king of the name of Pravarasena having four times performed the sacrifice of aswamedha. Distinct mention of this is made in the title deed of the gift of land, which he made to a Brahmana of the name of Devasarmacharya.

Thus :—

चतुरश्वमेधयाजिनः विष्णुवृद्धसगोत्रस्य सम्राजः वाकाटकानां महाराजश्रीप्रवरसेनस्य इत्यादि ।*

"King Pravarasena the performer of four sacrifices of "horse, descended from king Vishnu-rudra, the sovereign "of Kataka &c."

It is also mentioned in this title deed that the ancestors of Pravarasena ten times performed the sacrifice of horse.

Thus :—

दशाश्वमेधावभृथस्नातानाम् .*

"Performed ten times the sacrifice of horse."

"3290 years after the Kali-yuga has commenced, there will be a King on this earth of the name of Sudraka. He will be a great hero and one of the principal devotees. He will destroy all the sinful and potent sovereigns and contemplating and worshipping the Divinity at Charvita he will acquire success in Yoga (devotion). Twenty years after that, the descendants of the Nanda family will become sovereigns. Chanakya will destroy this Nanda family and comtemplating and worshipping the Divinity at Sukla-tirtha will expiate his sins. 690 years after that, Vikramaditya will become king."

* See P. 726 Asiatic Society's Journal Nov. 1836.

We have also evidence of Mihirakula, a king of Kasmira, having entered fire.

Thus :—

स वर्षसप्ततिं भुक्त्वा भुवं भूलोकभैरवः ।
भूरिरोगार्दितवपुः प्राविशज्जातवेदसम् ॥*

"Of fiery disposition, King Mihirakula, after enjoying "sovereignty for seventy years and being attacked with many "diseases, entered fire.

King Mihirakula led his army to Singhala (Ceylon) and deposed the sovereign of the Islands from his throne. From this, it is evident, that at his time sea-voyage was not considered as a prohibition.

Thus :—

स जातु देवीं संवीतसिंहलांशुककञ्चुकाम् ।
हेमपादाङ्कितकुचां दृष्ट्वा जज्वाल मन्युना ॥ 296.
सिंहलेषु नरेन्द्राङ्घ्रिमुद्राङ्कः क्रियते पटः ।
इति कञ्चुकिना पृष्टेनोक्तो यात्रां व्यधात्ततः ॥ 297.
स सिंहलेन्द्रेण समं संरम्भादुदपाटयत् ।
चिरेण चरणस्पृष्टमिवाशोकमसौ द्रुमम् ॥ 298. *

"The Queen had worn a bodice manufactured at Singhala.. "King Mihirakula, seeing foot marks in gold upon her "breast, was all inflamed with ire. On enquiring, the eu-

* Rajatarangini by Kahlana. Taranga I.

" nuch of the female apartments replied 'On clothes manufactured in Singhala they imprint the foot marks of their sovereign. On hearing this, the king marched to invade Singhala. King Mihirakula fought a battle with the king of Singhala and thus appeased the anger, which he felt from the circumstance of the foot marks of the latter having touched the breast of his queen."

There is clear evidence of king Jayapira having sent his ambassador to Singhala. This, therefore, is an additional proof, that it was usual then to undertake sea-voyages.

Thus :—

सान्धिविग्रहिकः सोऽथ गच्छन् पोतच्युतोऽम्बुधौ ।
ग्रासं प्राप्तं तिमिनाप्ति तिमिमुत्पाट्य निर्गतः ॥ 503.

"The ambassador fell into the sea from the vessel. A whale swallowed him up. He burst assunder its stomach and came out."

We find that Matrigupta, a king of Kasmira, adopted the Dharma of an ascetic.

Thus :—

अथ वाराणसीं गत्वा कृतकाषायसंग्रहः ।
सर्वं संन्यस्य सुकृती मातृगुप्तोऽभवद्यतिः ॥ 322. †

* Rajatarangini by Kahlana. Taranga IV.

† Rajatarangini by Kahlana. Taranga. III.

"Afterwards the pious and virtuous Matrigupta, giving "up every thing worldly, went to Benares and wearing red "clothes adopted the Dharma of an ascetic." *

King Suvastu in the year 1018 of the Sanvat, the era of Vikramaditya, erected a temple to Siva of the name of Harshadeva. In the tablet, which was attached to the temple, distinct mention is made of his having observed a life-long Brahmacharya.

Thus :—

आजन्मब्रह्मचारी दिगमलवसनः संयतात्मा तपस्वी
श्रीहर्षाराधनैकव्यसनशुभमतिस्त्यक्तसंसारमोहः ।
आसीद्यो दक्षदक्षा नवतरवपुषां वत्सः श्रीसुवस्तु-
र्येनेदं धर्म्मवित्तैः सुघटितविकटं कारितं हर्षहर्म्यम् ॥ †

"That Suvastu, who observed a life-long Brahmacharya, "remained naked, restrained his passions, led the life of a "hermit, was devoted to the worship of Harshadeva, was "devoid of all attachment to the infatuations of the world, had "accomplished the object of human existence, and was a "handsome person, has for pious purposes erected the well "constructed and the vast temple of Harshadeva."

आसीच्छैवः शिवभक्तो यो हीमपाशुपतव्रतः ।†

"He observed a life-long Brahmacharya and was a devoted Sivite."

* Even in the present age, it is usual for persons, in all parts of India, to become ascetic.

† See P. 378 Asiatic Society's Journal, July 1835.

From all this, it clearly appears that the sacrifice of horse, distant pilgrimage, entrance into fire, the adoption of the life of an ascetic, Sea-voyage, Brahmacharya of long duration, and the marriage of wedded women, are the Dharmas which have been observed in the Kali-yuga. There is not the least doubt that the Hindus of the olden times had greater knowledge of Sastras and had entertained a greater veneration for them than those of the Kali-yuga. They however, without observing the prohibition of the Adi Purana &c., used to perform the sacrifice of horse, entered the fire, and so on. From this, it is clearly proved, that the Hindus of those ages did not desist from the exercise of the actions which had the sanction of the Smritis, from the mere circumstance of their performance being prohibited in the Puranas. It is stated in the Aditya Purana, that

एतानि लोकगुप्त्यर्थं कलेरादौ महात्मभिः ।
निवर्त्तितानि कर्म्माणि व्यवस्थापूर्व्वकं बुधैः ॥

"These (that is Aswamedha &c.) have been legally abrogated, in the beginning of the Kali-yuga, by the wise and "magnanimous, for the protection of men."

and for confirming what the wise and magnanimous have said, it is stated at last, that

समयश्चापि साधूनां प्रमाणं वेदवद्भवेत् ।

"The decision of the virtuous is authority like the Vedas."

When in the face of this dictum, the Hindus of olden times used to perform the Aswamedha, without minding the prohibitions of the Puranas, there is not the least doubt, that these prohibitions were neither considered nor respected as such. Besides, there is a prohibition in the Aditya Purana of the filiation of any other sons than the Dattaka (son given) and the Aurasa (son of the body). But the inhabitants of Benares and the neighbouring districts are in the practice of taking Kritrima sons. It is for this, that Nanda Pandita, in his Dattaka Mimansa, has decided, that

दत्तवद् कृत्रिमस्याप्युपलक्षणम् औरसः क्षेत्रजश्चैव दत्तः
कृत्रिमकः सुत इति कलिधर्मप्रस्तावे पराशरस्मरणात्।

"On the failure of the son of the body, like Dattaka we "can take also a Kritrima son; because, Parasara has or- "dained that in the Kali-yuga, there should be three sorts "of sons, the Aurasa, the Dattaka and Kritrima."

That is, though according to the prohibition of the Aditya Purana, there could, in the Kali-yuga, be but two classes of sons, the Dattaka and the Aurasa, yet when Parasara, in declaring the Dharmas of Kali, has sanctioned the filiation of the Kritrima, this latter also becomes canonical. Distant pilgrimage, we find, is mentioned as a prohibition in the Aditya Purana. But it is unknown to none that even now many persons go on distant pilgrimages. The prohibition of the rule of expiation for Brahmanas extending to death is a prohibition without having ever been observed; for the celebrated Udayanacharya, who defeated (in controversy) the Buddhists and established on a firm basis the Vaidic religion, ended his life by burning himself to death. Very lately, a distinguished personage*, with the view of expiating his sins, observed the rule of expiation extending to death and starved himself till his life ended, with the sanction of all the Pandits of Benares.

When, therefore, Parasara has given his sanction to the performance of the sacrifice of horse with reference to the Kali-yuga, and when clear evidence is found of kings at different periods of the Kali-yuga having performed the sacrifice, it becomes a Dharma which may be observed in the Kali in common with the other Yugas. The shortening of the period of Asaucha (impurity) similarly, when mentioned in the Parasara-sanhita as a Dharma of the Kali, becomes such without a shadow of doubt. The reason, however, why we do not see the Brahmanas of the modern times shorten their periods of impurity, is that Parasara has given his precept for the shortening of this impurity with reference to them alone, who perform every day sacrifices at the alter and who every day study the Vedas.

Thus:—

एकाहात् शुध्यते विप्रो योऽग्निवेदसमन्वितः ।
त्र्यहात् केवलवेदस्तु विहीनो दशभिर्दिनैः ॥

"The Brahmana, who performs every day sacrifices at "the alter and every day studies the Vedas, shall be cleared "of impurity in one day, and he, who simply studies the "vedas, in three days. He, who neither performs the one

* The late Samachurn Banerjea.

"nor studies the other, shall be cleared of impurity in ten
"days."

Since, now a days, every-day sacrifice and the study of the Vedas have fallen into disuse, the shortening of the period of impurity has in consequence been disused. And when in the Parasara Sanhita the eating of the *Anna* (edibles), offered by a Dasa, Napita and Gopala &c. of the Sudra caste, has been mentioned as a Dharma of the Kali-yuga, that it is such there cannot be the least doubt. It might be urged, that if according to Parasara, the eating of the edibles, of a Dasa &c. in the Kali-yuga be allowable, are the three superior castes (the Brahmans, Kshatriyas and Vaisyas) then allowed to eat the *anna* of those Sudras? I think they are allowed to eat and they do generally eat. A careful consideration of the purport of the Text in which Parasara gives this permission and of the two Texts that precede, shall make even my opponents agree to this.

Thus :—

शुष्कान्नं गोरसं स्नेहं शूद्रवेश्मन आगतम्।
पक्वं विप्रगृहे पूतं भोज्यं तन्मनुरब्रवीत्॥

"Dried edibles, that is unboiled rice; cowjuice, that is
"milk, and oil, when brought from the house of a Sudra and
"cooked at the house of a Brahmana, becomes purified and
"Manu has declared that *anna* (edibles) to be acceptable
"as food."

This Text states that a Brahmana may, without incurring guilt, bring to his home unboiled rice &c. given to him by a Sudra, and eat them after having them cooked at his own house. It is inferentially to be understood, therefore, that he incurs guilt by eating them, after having them cooked at a Sudra's house.

आपत्काले तु विप्रेण भुक्तं शूद्रगृहे यदि ।
मनस्तापेन शुध्येत द्रुपदां वा शतं जपेत् ॥

"At the time of danger, if a Brahmana eats at the house "of a Sudra, he will be cleared of all impurity by repen-"tance, or by repeating the Drupada Mantra a hundred "times."

That eating at the time of danger at a Sudra's house, after cooking the edibles there, is not reprehensible, clearly appears from this Text. It is inferentially evident, therefore, that eating at a Sudra's house after cooking the edibles there, at other times than those of danger, is reprehensible.

दासनापितगोपालकुलमित्रार्द्धसीरिणः ।
एते शूद्रेषु भोज्यान्ना यश्चात्मानं निवेदयेत् ॥

"Of the Sudra caste, Dasa, Napita, Gopala, Kulamitra, "and Ardhasiri are the classes, and those that come for "help are the individuals, whose *anna* may be eaten; that "is, the unboiled rice &c., which they might offer, may be "eaten, after being boiled or cooked at their houses."

By these three Texts it is clear, that if a Brahmana eats even the unboiled rice &c., offered by a Sudra, after cooking them at his (the Sudra's) house, he eats the *anna* of a Sudra; the unboiled rice &c., given by a

Sudra, do not become the *Anna* of a Sudra, when brought home and eaten after being cooked. At times of danger however, these edibles might be eaten at a Sudra's house after cooking them there. But the unboiled rice given by a Dasa, Napita, or a Gopala and so forth may, without incurring guilt, be eaten after cooking or boiling it at his house, whether at times of danger or at other times.

Now let my readers judge what harm is there in accepting this sort of *anna* of a Sudra. Some have understood the word Sudranna (anna of a Sudra) to mean the boiled rice of a Sudra. This, however, cannot be the meaning of the word here. Had it been so, there would not have been in the Aditya Purana the prohibition of the cooking of the *anna* of a twice born by any one of the Sudra caste, immediately after the prohibition of the eating of the *anna* of Dasa, Napita &c. of the Sudra's.* When, of the two prohibitions, one after the other, in the one that comes last, the cooking of the *anna* is distinctly mentioned, the first prohibition, as a matter of course, must refer to uncooked *anna*. It must be considered also that even unboiled rice of the Sudras is treated in the Sastras as Sudranna.

शूद्रेषु दासगोपालकुलमित्रार्द्धसीरिणाम् ।
भोज्यान्नता गृहस्थस्य तीर्थसेवातिदूरतः ॥
ब्राह्मणादिषु शूद्रस्य पक्वतादिक्रियापि च ।

"The eating of the *anna* by a grihastha (householder) of the twice born classes offered to him by a Dasa, Gopala, Kulamitra, and Ardhasiri of the Sudra caste; distant pilgrimage; the cooking of a Brahmana's *anna* by a Sudra (are prohibited in the Kali-yuga).

Thus :—

आमं शूद्रस्य पक्वान्नं पक्वमुच्छिष्टमुच्यते ।*

"The unboiled *anna* of a Sudra is to be considered as boil-"ed ; the boiled *anna* of a Sudra as an offal."

The explanation that has been given above of the word Sudranna is corroborated by a discussion on the subject by the Smarta Bhattacharya Raghunandana.

Thus :—

आमान्नं दत्तमपि भोजनकाले तद्गृहावस्थितं शूद्रान्नम् । तथाचाङ्गिराः

शूद्रवेश्मनि विप्रेण क्षीरं वा यदि वा दधि ।
निवृत्तेन न भोक्तव्यं शूद्रान्नं तदपि स्मृतम् ॥

निवृत्तेन शूद्रान्नान्निवृत्तेन । अपि शब्दात् आमात् घृततण्डुलादि । स्वगृहागते पुनरङ्गिराः

यथा यतस्ततो ह्यापः शुद्धिं यान्ति नदीं गताः ।
शूद्राद्विप्रगृहेष्वन्नं प्रविष्टन्तु सदा शुचि ॥

प्रविष्टेऽपि स्वीकारापेक्षामाह पराशरः

तावद्भवति शूद्रान्नं यावन्न स्पृशति द्विजः ।
द्विजातिकरसंस्पृष्टं सर्वं तद्धविरुच्यते ॥

स्पृशति स्वीकरोतीति कल्पतरुः । तत्र सम्प्रोक्ष्य ग्राह्यमाह विष्णुपुराणम्

सम्प्रोक्ष्य विधिना स्वीकुर्यात् शूद्रान्नं स्वगृहागतम् ।

* Tithitattwa. Durgapujatattwa.

यच्च पात्रान्तरेण ग्राह्यमाहाङ्गिराः

स्वपात्रे यच्च विन्यस्तं दुग्धं यच्छति नित्यशः ।

पात्रान्तरगतं ग्राह्यं दुग्धं स्वगृह आगतम् ॥

एतेषु स्वगृह आगतस्यैव शुद्धत्वं शूद्रगृहगतस्य शूद्रान्नदोषभागित्वं प्रतीयते ।

"Even unboiled rice offered by a Sudra and eaten at his "house becomes Sudranna; for Angira has said, that 'A "Brahmana, who has ceased eating Sudranna, should not "drink even milk or curd at a Sudra's house, for that also "is Sudranna.' On the subject of unboiled rice &c., Angira "has said again, that 'As water, coming from any part, "becomes purified the moment it has fallen into the river, so "unboiled rice &c. on their very entrance from a Sudra's "house to a Brahmana's, becomes purified.' Parasara has "said that Sudranna, even after it has entered a Brahmana's "house, in order to be purified, requires his acceptance: "thus—'So long as a Brahmana does not accept it, it re-"mains Sudranna; a touch of his hand purifies it.' In the "Vishnu Purana, it has been stated that Sudranna should "be accepted after being washed or sprinkled with water: "thus—'When Sudranna comes to one's own house, it should "be accepted after being sprinkled.' Angira has stated "that Sudranna is to be received on a different plate from "that on which it is brought: thus—'The milk or curd "which a Sudra makes a gift of, on his own plate, when "brought to one's own house, should be accepted after being "placed on a different plate.' From these, it is demonstrated "that unboiled rice &c. given by a Sudra lose all impurity "when brought to one's own house; when they remain at a "Sudra's, they have the impurity of Sudranna."

From all these considerations, therefore, it is evident that starting from the preconceived notion that the sacrifice of horse &c. are not the Dharmas of the Kali-yuga, it is no way consistent with reason to come to the conclusion, that because these Dharmas are sanctioned in the Parasara Sanhita, Parasara has not only declared the Dharmas of the Kali-yuga, but has also declared those of others, and that consequently Parasara *S*anhita does not teach the Dharmas of the Kali-yuga alone.

CHAPTER. XX.

THE FATHER CAN MAKE A GIFT OF HIS WIDOWED DAUGHTER.

Many have stated the question, in the form of an objection, " that in marriage, who is to make the gift of a widow ? When the father has once given her away, his right in her has ceased. When he has no right in her, how can he dispose of her by giving her again to ano ther in marriage ?"

We have at present in our country two sorts of marriage " the Brahma" and "Asura," that is by a gift or sale of the daughter. Here the words "gift" and "sale" do not exactly mean what they mean elsewhere. In ordinary cases, a man can make a gift or sale of a thing, if he has a right in it. He loses his right in that thing, if he once makes a sale or gift of it, and consequently cannot make a sale or gift of it again. From time immemorial, this law prevails with reference to the gift or sale of land, house, garden, cattle &c. There seems, however, to be no analogy between such sale or gift, and sale or gift of a daughter. In the case of land, cattle &c. no one can make a gift or sale, if he has no right therein. Should he happen to make such a gift or sale, it becomes null and void. But this rule does not hold with reference to the gift of a daughter. Gift in marriage is not actual but merely nominal. The framers of our Sastras have enjoined the disposal of the daughter in marriage under the designation of gift. The marriage is consummated on any one's making this gift. The marriage is valid and complete by the gift of the bride by a person who could have no right whatsoever in her, equally with her gift by him who may have an actual right in her. In the case of ordinary things, no person can make over by gift a thing to another when he has no right in that thing, while a bride can be made over in gift by any person of the same caste.

Thus—

पिता दद्यात् स्वयं कन्यां भ्राता वानुमतः पितुः ।
मातामहो मातुलश्च सकुल्यो बान्धवस्तथा ॥
माता त्वभावे सर्वेषां प्रकृतौ यदि वर्त्तते ।
तस्यामप्रकृतिस्थायां कन्यां दद्युः स्वजातयः ॥*

"The father should himself make the gift of the daughter, " or the brother should do so with the permission of the fa-

* Narada-sanhita, quoted in the Udvahatattwa.

"ther. The maternal grand father, the maternal uncle, "persons descended from the same paternal ancestor, and "persons with whom there are ties of consanguinity, shall "make the gift of the bride. In the absence of all these, the "mother, if she is in her sane state, shall make the gift, "if she is not, the gift shall be made by persons of the same "caste."

Mark now, if it had been the intention of the framers of our Sastras, that the same rule shall hold with reference to the gift of a bride as with reference to the gift of land, cattle &c., that is, he alone who has a right in her shall be entitled to make the gift, then how could persons of the same caste be entitled to make the gift? If any one has a right in her it is her father and mother alone. The others can have a right in her by no possibility. If the rule had been, that like the gift of land, cattle &c., the gift of a bride shall be made by him alone who has a right in her, then the framers of the Sastras would not have stated the maternal grand father &c. as persons entitled to make the gift, or why would they make the mother the person last entitled to make the gift? She should have been, in that case, held second to the father only. In fact, there cannot be the same right in a daughter as there is in land, cattle &c.; if there had been, the giving away of a bride in marriage without the knowledge and consent of the father, by any other person, would have been considered null and void, being a gift by a person who had no right whatsoever. But it is not a rare occurrence, that sometimes persons give away females in marriage, under such circumstances.

Why are such marriages valid? Why cannot the father lay complaints before a court of justice, and make void the gift of his daughter by a person who had no right whatsoever in her? The gift of another's land and cattle is never valid. It becomes void when a complaint is lodged before a court of justice. From all these considerations, therefore, the gift of a bride is merely nominal and is founded on no right whatsoever. If then the gift of a daughter is founded on no right whatsoever in her, and if it is a gift merely nominal and is enjoined by the Sastras as only a part of the marriage ceremony, there is nothing to prevent the father to give her away in marriage again, if her husband is dead, or in any other contingencies specified in the Sastras. As in the Text quoted above, sanction is given to the gift of a female on her first marriage,. so in other Texts like sanction is given, in certain contingencies, to the gift of her on her remarriage.

Thus:—

> स तु यद्यन्यजातीयः पतितः क्लीव एव च।
> विकर्मस्थः सगोत्रो वा दासो दीर्घामयोऽपि वा।
> ऊढापि देया सान्यस्मै सहावरणभूषणा॥

"If after wedding, the husband be found to be of a different caste, degraded, impotent, unprincipled, of the same Gotra or family, a slave, or a valetudinarian, then a married woman should be bestowed upon another decked with proper apparel and ornaments."

Mark! sanction is here give to *give* away *again* a wedded female in marriage in due form. If the circumstance of having given away a daughter once in marriage were a bar to her being made a gift of on the occasion of remarriage, then the great sage Katyayana would not have given clear sanction to her being made over to another as a gift, on her husband being found to be degraded, impotent, valetudinarian &c. Moreover, it is not only that we find a mere sanction, but clear evidence is found that a father *did make* the gift of a widowed daughter on the occasion of her remarriage.

Thus—

अर्ज्जुनस्यात्मजः श्रीमानिरावान्नाम वीर्य्यवान्।
सुतायां नागराजस्य जातः पार्थेन धीमता॥
ऐरावतेन सा दत्ता ह्यनपत्या महात्मना।
पत्यौ हते सुपर्णेन कृपणा दीनचेतना॥

" By Arjuna was begotten on the daughter of the Nag-raja, " a handsome and powerful son named Iravan. When her " husband was killed by Suparna, Airavata, the magnanimous " king of the Nagas, made a gift of that dejected, sorrow-" stricken, childless daughter to Arjuna."

When, therefore, the gift of a daughter is, as proved above, not founded on right, but only forms a part of the marriage ceremony, when there is clear sanction in the Sastras to make the gift of a daughter on the occasion of her remarriage with all the rites and ceremonies of marriage, and when we have clear evidence of a widowed daughter having been made over as a gift on the occasion of her remarriage; the objection that, after the gift of the daughter, the father has lost all his right in her and therefore cannot give her away a second time in marriage, is altogether unreasonable. The fact is, those parties, who are entitled, according to the Sastras, to make the gift of a female on the occasion of her first marriage, can also do so on the occasion of her remarriage.

CHAPTER XXII.

The Mantras (Nuptial Texts) to be used on the occasion of a Second Marriage are the same, as those that are used on the occasion of a First Marriage.

Some of the Replicants object to the remarriage of widows on the ground, that there are no Mantras for such marriage,. and that therefore it cannot be contracted. This seems to be a futile objection. There is nothing in the Mantras used on the occasion of a first marriage to make it valid, which would prevent their being used on the occasion of a second. Those Mantras, that sanctify the first matrimonial connexion, shall also sanctify the second.

It has already been indisputably established that Manu, Vishnu, Vasishtha, Yajnavalkya, Narada, and Katyayana have enjoined the remarriage of women under certain contingencies. But if the Mantras, prescribed for the first marriages, had not been applicable to remarriages, those Rishis would certainly have prescribed other Mantras for them, as no marriage is valid without Mantras. When, however, there are no such separate Mantras, the sanction of the Rishis for remarriage would be absurd, if the Mantras for the first marriage were not applicable to the second. The *mere intercourse* of the sexes can never be called the *Sanskara* (rite) *of marriage*, which requires the application of proper Mantras in due form. If the *remarriage* of women were *mere intercourse* with men, not duly sanctified by proper Mantras, the authors of our Sastras aforesaid would not have applied the word *Sanskara* to it also. Thus,

Manu says :—

या पत्या वा परित्यक्ता विधवा वा स्वयेच्छया ।
उत्पादयेत् पुनर्भूत्वा स पौनर्भव उच्यते ॥ 9. 175.
सा चेदक्षतयोनिः स्याद्गतप्रत्यागतापि वा ।
पौनर्भवेण भर्त्रा सा पुनः संस्कारमर्हति ॥ 9. 176.

" If a woman after becoming a widow, or being divorced " by her husband, marries again, the son born of her of this " marriage, is called a Paunarbhava. If she be a virgin, " or if she leave her husband and return to him, she is again " entitled to the *Sanskara* or ceremony of marriage."

Vasishtha says :—

पाणिग्रहे मृते बाला केवलं मन्त्रसंस्कृता ।
सा चेदक्षतयोनिः स्यात् पुनः संस्कारमर्हति ॥ Ch. 17.

"She, who is married but continues a virgin, is again entitled to the *Sanskara*, if her husband dies."

Vishnu says :—

अक्षता भूयः संस्कृता पुनर्भूः । Ch. 15.

"She, who, though married, continues a virgin and undergoes the *Sanskara* for a second time, is called Punarbhu."

Yajnavalkya says :—

अक्षता च क्षता चैव पुनर्भूः संस्कृता पुनः । 1. 67.

"She, who continues a virgin, or otherwise, is called Punarbhu, if she undergoes the *Sanskara* for a second time."

When, therefore, Manu, Vishnu, Vasishtha, Yajnavalkya, Parasara and other writers of our Sastras, have enjoined the remarriage of women under certain contingencies; when they have denominated such marriage "the *Sanskara of marriage*"; when the word *Sanskara* can by no means be applied to a *mere intercourse* of the sexes, not sanctified by Mantras; when they have legalized the issue of such marriages; and when, at the same time, they have not prescribed a different set of Mantras for them, the Mantras, now used in first marriages, should certainly be used in the second, especially as there is nothing in those Mantras which would make them inapplicable to remarriage of females.

Some of the oppositionists contend for the inapplicability of the existing Mantras to remarriage of women on the strength of the following Text of Manu :—

पाणिग्रहणिका मन्त्राः कन्यास्वेव प्रतिष्ठिताः ।
नाकन्यासु क्वचिन्नृणां लुप्तधर्म्मक्रिया हि ताः ॥ 8. 226.

"The nuptial Texts are applied solely to *Kanyas* or vir-"gins, and nowhere to *Akanyas* or girls who have lost their "virginity; *since they are excluded from the performance of "religious duties.*"

Here I have to observe that in the Text, above cited, Manu, by the word *Akanya*, does uot mean *widows* but girls who have lost their virginity before marriage by illicit intercourse with men, as is evident from the last part of the clause "*Since they are excluded from the performance of religious duties.*" No Hindu can assert that widows are excluded from those duties. On the contrary, such widows, who would prefer widowhood to remarriage, are enjoined by the Sastras to pass their lives in the performance of such duties.

CHAPTER XIII.

IN MATRIMONIAL ALLIANCES UNMARRIED DAMSELS ARE PREFERABLE TO MARRIED ONES IN THE SAME WAY AS UNMARRIED MEN ARE TO MARRIED ONES.

While dwelling upon the subject of the remarriage of widows, it should be considered that the following Text of Yajnavalkya enjoins marriage with an unmarried girl:

अविप्लुतब्रह्मचर्यो लक्षण्यां स्त्रियमुद्वहेत् ।
अनन्यपूर्विकां कान्तामसपिण्डां यवीयसीम् ॥*

" After leading the life of a student in the Vedas, a person " should marry an unmarried, amiable damsel, inferior in " age, with auspicious physical signs, and without the pale " of consanguinity."

From this as well as other Texts upon the subject, the oppositionists try to establish that a married damsel should not be married again.

This conclusion is no way cosistent with the precept of Manu, Yajnavalkya, Vasishtha, Vishnu, and other sages, who have in their Sanhitas given sanction, in certain contingencies, to the remarriage of married women. For, if the conclusion of my adversaries be admitted, the sanction of the sages alluded to becomes absurd. In fact the true purport of the Text is, that when a person is entering into matrimonial alliance, he should prefer an unmarried bride to a married one, just as in the bestowal of a daughter, an unmarried person should be preferred to a married one. As in the Text of Yajnavalkya a man is enjoined to marry an unmarried damsel, so in the following Text of Baudhayana it is laid down that a daughter should be bestowed on an unmarried man :

श्रुतशीलिने विज्ञाय ब्रह्मचारिणेऽर्थिने देया ॥†

" A daughter should be bestowed on a suitor studied in " the Vedas, virtuous, wise and *unmarried*."

* Yajnavalkya-sanhita. 1. 52.

† Quoted in the Udvahatattwa and Yajnavalkya Dipakalika.

If from this we infer that the bestowal of a daughter on a person once married is altogether prohibited, the inference would jar with other Texts in which we find, that on the demise of a wife, on her barrenness, or under other contingencies, male persons are permitted to marry again. To reconcile this apparent discrepancy, we must conclude that the Texts refer to different degrees of preference. A similar conclusion must be arrived at with regard to the marrying a virgin or a married damsel. In fact marrying a damsel once married is as much a case of second preference on the part of a man, as marrying a male person once married is on the part of woman.

This is a conclusion which has been arrived at by the Smartta Bhattacharya Raghunandana also.

Thus :—

बौधायनः श्रुतशीलिने विज्ञाय ब्रह्मचारिणेऽर्थिने देया। ब्रह्मचारिणे अजातस्त्रीसम्पर्कायेति कल्पतरुवाचस्पतिमिश्रदीपकलिके। जातस्त्रीसम्पर्कस्य द्वितीयविवाहे विवाहाष्टकबहिर्भावापत्तेस्तदुपादानं प्राशस्त्यार्थमिति तत्त्वम्॥*

"Baudhayana has said that a daughter should be bestowed "on a suitor studied in the Vedas, virtuous, wise and *un-*"*married*. From a too literal interpretation of this, it "would appear that daughters should be bestowed on *un-*"*married persons only*, and that the remarriage of a man once "married does not fall within any of the eight classes of "marriage. We are to understand, therefore, that by the use "of the adjective '*unmarried*' Baudhayana has meant that

* Udvahatattwa.

"the bestowal of a daughter on an *unmarried* person is a "*case of first preference.*"

In fact, a little observation would show, that the framers of the Sastras have on such matters laid down equal rules for both the sexes.—They have ordained that, before betrothment, inquiry as to the family and character of the bridegroom is as much necessary as that of the bride.* After the marriage is contracted, they make

* अविप्लुतब्रह्मचर्यो लक्षण्यां स्त्रियमुद्वहेत् ।
अनन्यपूर्विकां कान्तामसपिण्डां यवीयसीम् ॥ 1. 52.
अरोगिणीं भ्रातृमतीमसमानार्षगोत्रजाम् ।
पञ्चमात् सप्तमादूर्ध्वं मातृतः पितृतस्तथा ॥ 1. 53.
दशपुरुषविख्यातात् श्रोत्रियाणां महाकुलात् ।
स्फीतादपि न सञ्चारिरोगदोषसमन्वितात् ॥ 1. 54.
एतैरेव गुणैर्युक्तः सवर्णः श्रोत्रियो वरः ।
यत्नात् परीक्षितः पुंस्त्वे युवा धीमान् जनप्रियः ॥ 1. 55.

"After leading the life of a student in the Vedas, a person should "marry a damsel, unmarried, amiable, with auspicious physical signs, "inferior in age, without the pale of consanguinity, having no incurable "disease, having a brother, not descended from the same line of ancestors, and five degrees without the mother's side and seven without "the father's. A bride should not be selected from the family which has "a blemish or is subject to contagious disease notwithstanding it be very "distinguished, celebrated for ten generations, possessed of riches, corn "&c., and one in which the Vedas are every day studied. The bridegroom "also should be possessed of these attributes, should belong to the "same caste and should be an every day student of the Vedas. Moreover "every care should be taken to ascertain whether the bridegoom "is possessed of *Potency*. It is necessary also that he should be "youthful, intelligent and amiable." *Yajnavalkya.*

it as much a duty of the husband to please the wife, as that of the wife to please him.* Want of chastity they make as sinful on the part of man as on that of woman† As they have ordained man to marry again on the demise of his wife or on her proving barren &c., so they have ordained woman to marry again on the demise of her husband or on his proving impotent &c. Marrying a woman once married they have made as much a case of second preference on the part of man, as marrying a man once married on the part of woman.—But unfortunately

सन्तुष्टो भार्य्यया भर्त्ता भर्त्रा भार्य्या तथैव च।
यस्मिन्नेव कुले नित्यं कल्याणं तत्र वै ध्रुवम्॥ 3. 60.

"Constant prosperity attends the family in which the wife pleases "the husband and the husband pleases the wife." *Manu.*

यत्रानुकूल्यं दम्पत्योस्त्रिवर्गस्तत्र वर्द्धते॥ 1. 74.

"The family, in which the wife and the husband keep each other "pleased, and behave well towards each other, is one in which virtue, "riches and enjoyment increase." *Yajnavalkya.*

† व्युच्चरन्त्याः पतिं नार्य्या अद्यप्रभृति पातकम्।
भ्रूणहत्यासमं घोरं भविष्यत्यसुखावहम्।
भार्य्यां तथा व्युच्चरतः कौमारब्रह्मचारिणीम्।
पतिव्रतामेतदेव भविता पातकं भुवि॥

"Henceforward, a woman that will transgress her husband shall incur "the deep guilt of fœticide. And the husband that will transgress "a wife well-behaved and chaste, shall incur the same guilt." Mahabharata, Adi Parva, Ch. cxxii.

man, the stroger sex, arrogates to himself rights which he is not willing to accede to weak woman. He has taken the Sastras into his own hands and interprets and moulds them in a way which best suits his convenience; perfectly regardless of the degraded condition to which woman has been reduced through his selfishness and injustice. A sight of the wrongs of the women of modern India is really heart-rending. To respect the female sex and to make them happy are things almost unknown in this country. Nay men, who consider themselves wise and are esteemed as such by others, take a pleasure in the degraded state of the females.

Manu has declared :—

पितृभिर्भ्रातृभिश्चैताः पतिभिर्देवरैस्तथा ।
पूज्या भूषयितव्याश्च बहुकल्याणमीप्सुभिः ॥ 3. 55.
यत्र नार्यस्तु पूज्यन्ते रमन्ते तत्र देवताः ।
यत्रैतास्तु न पूज्यन्ते सर्वास्तत्राफलाः क्रियाः ॥ 3. 56.
शोचन्ति जामयो यत्र विनश्यत्याशु तत् कुलम् ।
न शोचन्ति तु यत्रैता वर्द्धते तद्धि सर्वदा ॥ 3. 57.
जामयो यानि गेहानि शपन्त्यप्रतिपूजिताः ।
तानि कृत्याहतानीव विनश्यन्ति समन्ततः ॥ 3. 58.

"Fathers, brothers, husbands, brothers of husband &c., "who wish for happiness and prosperity, should respect women 'and keep them adorned in clothes and ornaments. The "gods remain propitious to the family, in which the females "are respected. Sacrifices and gifts are productive of no "fruits in the family, in which women are not respected.

"The family soon goes to destruction, in which the females "are not respected. The family, in which the females are "happy, always rises in happiness and wealth. When, not "being properly treated and respected, women curse fami- "lies, the latter utterly perish, as if destroyed by Kritya."

Unfortunately this salutary rule regarding the treatment of women is scarcely followed; and the evil consequences, usually attendant upon a transgression of such a golden rule, are everywhere visible.

CHAPTER XXIV.

THE CUSTOM OF THE COUNTRY IS NOT A STRONGER AUTHORITY THAN THE SASTRAS.

I have, to the best of my ability, explained the true meaning and purport of the Texts quoted by the Replicants with the object to prove the nonconformity of the marriage of widows to the Sastras. I will now endeavour to meet another objection which they have made with regard to the introduction of the practice. The opponents have urged that even if the remarriage of widows be consonant to the Sastras, it should not prevail, being opposed to the custom of the country. Anticipating such an objection, I pointed out in my first pamphlet a Text from Vasishtha, to shew that the Sastra is a

* A Female Deity, to whom sacrifices are offered for the destruction of an enemy.

stronger authority than custom. But as I imagine that only one Text has not been considered sufficient by my opponents, I will cite other authorities on the subject.

Thus :—

धर्म्मं जिज्ञासमानानां प्रमाणं परमं श्रुतिः ।
द्वितीयं धर्म्मशास्त्रन्तु तृतीयं लोकसंग्रहः ॥*

" Those that wish to know what Dharmas are, for them " the Veda is the highest authority, the Smriti the second, " and Custom the third."

Here we see that custom is held as the weakest authority ; and the Veda and the Smriti are stronger authorities :

Again :

न यत्र साक्षाद्विधयो न निषेधाः श्रुतौ स्मृतौ ।
देशाचारकुलाचारैस्तत्र धर्म्मो निरूप्यते ॥†

" Where there are no direct sanctions or prohibitions laid " down in the Veda or the Smriti, the Dharmas are to be " ascertained from an observation of the custom of the coun- " try and of the family."

Thus it is distinctly stated that custom is to be followed on those matters only on which there are no precepts in the Sastras.

Further :

श्रुतिस्मृतिविरोधे तु परित्यागो यथा भवेत् ।

* Mahabharata, Anusasana Parva.

† Skanda Purana.

तथैव लौकिकं वाक्यं स्मृतिबाधे परित्यजेत् ॥*

"As Smriti is not to be accepted when it is opposed to the "Vedas, so custom is not to be respected when it is at vari- "ance with Smriti."

So when Smriti and custom are opposed to each other, custom is not to be followed.

When we see, therefore, that there is distinct sanction in the Sastras for the marriage of widows, to attempt to establish that it should not prevail, because it is opposed to the custom of the country, is acting in direct opposition to the opinion and precept of the framers of our Sastras.

CHAPTER XXV.

CONCLUSION.

Every one, having the senses of sight and hearing, must acknowledge how intolerable are the hardships of our widows especially of those who have the misfortune to lose their husbands at an early age; and how baneful to society are the effects of the custom which excludes them from the privilege of marrying again. Reader! I beseech you to think seriously for a while upon the subject, and then to say whether we should continue slaves to such a custom, regardless of the precepts of our Sastras

* A Smriti quoted in the Prayogaparijata.

or should we throw off the yoke, and resting on those holy sanctions, introduce among ourselves the marriage of widows, and thus relieve those unfortunate creatures from their miseries. While forming your decision, you should bear in mind that the customs of our country are not immutable in their nature. No one can assert that they have never undergone any change. On the contrary, the present inhabitants of India would appear to be altogether a different race, were you to compare their customs with those that prevailed in days of old amongst their ancestors. One instance will suffice to illustrate the truth of this statement. It was considered a heinous offence in a Sudra, if, in ancient times, he durst be seated on the same carpet or mat with a Brahmana; but the Brahmanas of these days, like menial servants, content themselves with sitting on the carpet or mat, while the Sudra occupies a raised seat upon the same.*

* This custom is opposed to the Sastras. It is not only the Sudras and Brahmanas ignorant of the Sastras that follow this custom, but those Brahmanas and Sudras who are reputed as versed in them, act in accordance with it without compunction.

Manu has said :—

सहासनमभिप्रेप्सुरुत्कृष्टस्यापकृष्टजः ।
कट्यां कृताङ्को निर्वास्यः स्फिचं वास्यावकर्तयेत् ॥ 8. 28.

"If a sudra seats himself on the same seat with a Brahmana, his loins "should be branded with heated iron, and he should be banished or his "loins cut asunder."

Changes in our customs have taken place even within a recent period. The Vaidyas, from the time of Rajah Rajbullub, have commenced to reduce the period of their Asaucha (impurity) to fifteen days, and to wear the sacred thread. Before his time, the period of their Asaucha was a month, and they did not wear the sacred thread. Even now, there are families among the Vaidyas who stick to the old custom. Have these innovators and their descendants ever been treated as men degraded and having no claim to the privileges of their caste? Again, before the appearance of the Dattakachandrika, all Hindus in adopting sons were obliged, in order to make the adoption valid, to take them before the age of five, and to perform the rite of Churakarana (ceremony of Tonsure) on them. Since the publication of that work, if a son is adopted, in the case of a Brahmana, before the ceremony of the sacred thread, and in the case of a Sudra, before the marriageable age, he is still admitted to be within the proper limits of age, and his adoption considered as valid.

In these cases, new customs were adopted according to a new interpretation of the Sastras, not because they were absolutely needed by the society at large, but merely because they suited the convenience or caprice of certain individuals. For, if the Vaidyas did not reduce the period of their Asaucha, or wear a theard, or if sons were not adopted after five years of age, society could neither gain nor lose. But what an amount of misery and evil does the country sustain from the non-prevalence of the marriage of widows! Here you have a positive evil—evil of a magnitude passing our imagination to conceive. Now, if you could adopt customs that at best suited but your convenience, you should do any thing for the removal of this awful evil, when you have your Sastras most explicitly permitting your widows to marry again.

But I am not without my apprehensions that many among you at the very sound of the word "custom" will consider it sinful even to enquire if the change should take place. There are others again, who, though in their hearts agree to the measure, have not the courage even to say that it should be adopted, only because it is opposed to the customs of their country. O what a miserable state of things is this! Custom is the supreme ruler in this country: Custom is the supreme instructor: The rule of custom is the paramount rule: The precept of custom is the paramount precept.

What a mighty influence is thine, O custom! Inexpressible in words! With what absolute sway dost thou rule over thy votaries! Thou hast trampled upon the Sastras, triumphed over virtue, and crushed the power of discriminating right from wrong and good from evil! Such is thy influence, that what is no way conformable to the Sastras is held in esteem, and what is consonant to them is set at open defience. Through thy influence, men, lost to all sense of religion, and reckless in their conduct, are every where regarded as virtuous and enjoy all the privileges of society, only because they adhere to mere forms: while those truly virtuous and of unblemished conduct, if they disregard those forms and disobey thy authority, are considered as the most irreligious, despised as the most depraved, and cut off from society.

What a sad misfortune has befallen our Sastras! Their authority is totally disregarded. They, who pass their lives in the performance of those acts which the Sastras repeatedly prohibit as subversive of caste and relegion, are every where respected as pious and virtuous: while, the mere *mention* of the duties prescribed by the Sastras makes a man looked upon as the most irreligious and vicious. A total disregard of the Sastras and a careful observance of mere usages and external forms is the source of the irreristible stream of vice which overflows the country.

How miserable is the presant state of India! It was once known to nations as the land of virtue. But the blood dries up to think that it is now looked upon as the land of depravity, and that from the conduct of its present race of people. From a view of its present degradation it is vain to look for a speedy reformation.

Countrymen! how long will you suffer yourselves to be led away by illusions! Open your eyes for once and see, that India, once the land of virtue, is being overflooded with the stream of adultery and fœticide. The degradation to which you have sunk is sadly low. Dip into the spirit of your Sastras, follow its dictates, and you shall be able to remove the foul blot from the face of your country. But unfortunately you are so much under the domination of long established prejudice, so slavishly attached to custom and the usages and forms of society, that I am afraid you will not soon be able to assert your dignity and follow the path of rectitude. Habit has so darkened your intellect and blunted your feelings, that it is impossible for you to have compassion for your helpless widows. When led away by the impulse of passion, they violate the vow of widowhood, you are willing to connive at their conduct. Losing all sense of honor and religion, and from apprehensions of mere exposure in society, you are willing to help in the work of fœticide. But what a wonder of wonders! You are not willing to follow the dictates of your Sastras, to give them in marriage again, and thus to relieve them from their intoterable sufferings, and yourselves from miseries, crimes and vices. You perhaps imagine that with the loss of their husbands, your females lose their nature as human beings and are subject no longer to the influence of passions. But what instances occur at every step to show, how sadly you are mistaken. Alas! what fruits of poison you are gathering from the tree of life, from moral torpitude and a sad want of reflection. How greatly is this to be deplored! Where *men* are void of pity and compassion, of a perception of right and wrong, of good and evil, and where *men* consider the observance of mere forms as the highest of duties and the greatest of virtues, in such a country would that women were never born.

Woman! in India, thy lot is cast in misery!

TO THE HONORABLE THE LEGISLATIVE COUNCIL OF INDIA.

The Humble Petition of the Undersigned Inhabitants of Calcutta and the Lower Provinces of Bengal.

MOST RESPECTFULLY SHEWETH,

1. That your Petitioners have read with much concern the Draft of a Bill entitled. "A Bill to remove all legal obstacles to the marriage of Hindu Widows," which was read by your Honorable Council for the first time on the 17th November last, and for the second time, on the 19th January. Your Petitioners are aware from the printed papers of your Honorable Council, that the said Bill has been brought in, on the Petition of certain Hindus who desire that Widow Marriage should be legalized. Your Petitioners are also sensible that the principle of the said Bill is consonant with the social system of their English fellow subjects, and therefore is likely to be acceptible to your Honorable Council; yet your Petitioners cannot but feel it as a duty as well to themselves as Hindus as to their countrymen in general, to submit their objections to the proposed law.

2. The preamble to the Bill states that "whereas it is known that by the law as administered in the Civil Courts established in the territories in the possession and under the government of the East India Company, Hindu Widows with some exceptions are held to be, by reason of their having been once married, incapable of contracting a second valid marriage, and the offspring of such widows by any second marriage are held to be illegitimate and incapable of inheriting property; and whereas many Hindus believe that this imputed legal incapacity, although it is in accordance with established custom, is not in accordance with a true interpretation of the precepts of their religion, and desire that the

Civil law administered by the courts of justice, shall no longer prevent those Hindus who may be so minded from adopting a different custom in accordance with the dictates of their own consciences" &c.

3. Your Petitioners beg leave to observe that the remarriage of Hindu females is not only not in accordance with the established usages of Hindus, but is likewise repugnant to the precepts of their religion and the ordinations of Hindu law, from which all their social institutions have originated. Though there are different tribes of Hindus who speak different tongues, follow different codes of laws, wear different dresses, and have different customs and usages, yet they are all unanimous in reprehending the marriage of their widows, in consequence of its being against the positive injunctions of their law, and the interpretations of that law by different commentators of ancient and modern times. The *Yajur Veda* in the *Taithriya Sakha* declares that "as round a single *Yupa* (sacrificial post) two tethers can be tied, so one person can marry two wives. As one tether can not be tied round two *Yupas*, so one female can not marry two husbands." The most ancient and revered of our lawgivers, Menu, says in Chapter V. verse 161 that "a widow who from a wish to bear children, slights her deceased husband by marrying again, brings disgrace on herself here below, and shall be excluded from the seat of her lord." And also at the following verse, "issue begotten on a woman by any other than her husband, is here declared to be no progeny of hers; no more than a child, begotten on the wife of another man, belongs to the begetter; nor is a second husband allowed in any part of this code to a virtuous woman." The same authority further directs in Chapter IX. verses 64 and 65, that "by men of twice-born classes no widow or childless wife must be authorized to conceive by any other than her lord; for they who authorize her to conceive by any other, violate the primeval law. Such a commission to a brother or other near kinsman, is nowhere mentioned in the nuptial texts of the Veda; nor is the marriage of a widow even named in the laws concerning marriage." The *Mahabharut*, too, lays down that "a woman is to have only one husband upon whom she

must depend through her whole life." These ordinations in the highest sacred works of the Hindus, added to the long established custom and usage of the country against the marriage of widows, will, your Petitioners trust, weigh more in the estimation of your Honorable Council than the forced construction of any solitary text apparently in its favour, but quite unsupported by a single instance of such marriage having ever been legally contracted in any period of the annals of the Hindus. Your Honorable Council will thus perceive that the marriage of Hindu widows is not in accordance with the dictates of Hindu law, as it is stated in the preamble to the Bill for the removal of legal obstacles to such marriages.

4. Your Petitioners further beg leave to submit that the proposed law is also at variance with the several statutes of the British Parliament and the Regulations of the East India Company, by which the natives of this country have from time to time been assured, that their rights of marriage and inheritance shall not be disturbed or violated. Section 23 of Regulation I. of 1772 which was re-enacted in Section 15 of Regulation IV. of 1793, ordains that in all suits regarding succession, inheritance, marriage and caste and all religious usages and institutions, the Mehamedan law shall prevail in respect of Mehamedans and the Hindu law in regard to Hindus. This is also laid down in the 21st George III Chap. 70 Sections 17, 18 and 19. The 3rd and 4th William IV Chap. 85 Section 53 expressly provides that in making any law for the natives of this country a due regard should be had to their religion, customs, laws and usages. The more subsequent Regulation V of 1831 declares that cases relating to the marriage, succession and inheritance of Mehamedans shall be decided according to Mehamedan law, and those concerning the Hindus shall be adjudicated according to Hindu law. These repeated declarations of the British Parliament and the local Government have induced a firm belief that the natives of this country would be continued in the enjoyment of their laws relating to marriage, succession and inheritance. Even in the General Order recently issued by the Governor General in Council in

reference to the late disturbance at Bolarum and the conduct of Brigadier Mackenzie on the occasion, the public officers were enjoined in the strongest manner "never to interfere with the religious observances of the natives of India." When the late Law Commission in 1837 applied to the Sudder Courts at the several Presidencies for their opinions on the subject of Hindu Widow Marriage, the Judges of those Courts unanimously observed that the legalization of such marriage "would be an interference with the Hindus in the matter of their own law and religion and at once dislocate the whole frame work of Hindu jurisprudence." The Hindu Society has undergone no material change whatever since that year, which would warrant the Legislature to interfere with the Hindu law on the ground of expediency. Its integrity, it is true, has been most seriously affected by the enactment of Act XXI of 1850, but your Petitioners submit that one encroachment does not justify another; and, what is of more importance, the said law has not increased the number of native converts to Christianity. The experience of the last six years shows that practically it has been of no more use than affording an example of an arbitrary and uncalled-for interference with the Hindu law of inheritance. Legislative intervention has never yet been able to effect a change in public opinion, while the more such interference is exercised, the more it assumes an objectionable character.

5. Your Petitioners have been told that the Bill for the removal of legal obstacles to the marriage of Hindu widows, is merely a *permissive* law. In reply they beg leave to observe that so far as it allows a widow to contract a second marriage, at her option, it is undoubtedly of a permissive character, but in its immediate and ultimate consequences, when it interferes with the rights of others, your Petitioners humbly submit that it is a *compulsory* measure. As for example, if a Hindu dies leaving two daughters, both of whom are widows, but the one has a son, and the other no children; by the Hindu law of inheritance as it is now administered, that son will be the sole heir of his maternal grandfather. But if the childless widow contracts a second marriage

and has issue by her second husband, by the proposed law they would be entitled to equal shares of the property of their mother's father with the son of the widow, who has not remarried. Again, if a married woman dies, leaving two sons, who have acquired property. Their father marries a widow and dies leaving a son by her. One of the brothers has children while the other has not; but both of them subsequently die. By the Hindu law the said children will succeed to the whole of that property; but by the proposed law, the son of the widow will not only share equally with the two brothers at first, but will also succeed to the share of the deceased among them to the exclusion of the said children. Again, a person dies leaving a widow but no issue and directs her by his will to adopt a son and heir. If before the adoption takes place she contracts a second marriage, she cannot carry out the directions of her deceased husband according to Hindu law: and the consequence will be that his line will be extinct; that he and his ancestors will have none to perform the usual funeral ceremonies prescribed by the Hindu religion; and that whatever property he may have left, will go to his next of kin, who, by the proposed law, will find it to their interest to induce the widow to marry, and thus defeat the intentions of her first husband for their own benefit.

6. Your Petitioners can, to an unlimited extent, multiply instances in which the proposed law for the marriage of Hindu Widows will operate against the civil rights of others who may prefer to follow the laws and usages of their country,—a consequence which had no doubt been anticipated by the Judges of the several Sudder Courts, when they gave it as their opinion that the legalization of such marriage would amount to an interference with the customs and laws of the Hindus, and would at once upset their present system of jurisprudence. If the Petitioners in favour of Widow Marriage be disposed to adopt "a different custom in accordance with the dictates of their own consciences," as it is stated in the preamble to the Bill, your Petitioners have no objection whatever to their doing so, but when the law which they have asked for, inter-

feres with the rights of others, who entertain different opinions and are not inclined to follow their example, their demand is manifestly unjust and unreasonable. The Petitioners, at whose instance the proposed law has been brought in, form a very small and insignificant portion of the vast masses of the people whom your Petitioners represent. It would, therefore, be scarcely just and reasonable or even expedient to enact a law for the minority which shall interfere with the rights of the majority. As far as your Petitioners have been able to communicate with the people of the interior, during the short space of two months, which has elapsed between the first and second reading of the Bill, they have found but one opinion exist among all classes of men, and that opinion is, your Petitioners need hardly say, against the proposed law; and if the fact of that law being under the consideration of your Honorable Council be made known still more extensively, your Petitioners are sure the general voice of the entire Hindu population will be raised against its enactment. The great majority of the people of this country have yet had no intimation of the proceedings which have been held in respect of the Bill for the legalization of the marriage of Hindu Widows. They have no knowledge of the English language, and do not read the English newspapers in which the reports of your Honorable Council appear. The Bill made its appearance in the Bengallee *Government Gazette* only on the 12th February; but still that would not be sufficient, as the Bengallee language is only read and understood in only one of the provinces out of the immense extent of territories subject to British rule in India, and that, too, by a comparatively small portion of its inhabitants. Its enactment will, therefore, be without the knowledge of the people whose interests are to be affected by it. If they know of it, your Petitioners are certain they would object to it, and it would be unwise to pass it into law on the application of a few against the wishes of the hundred thousands of the Hindus who own allegiance to the British Crown in India.

7. Your Petitioners also beg leave to submit that the proposed law for the legalization of Hindu Widow Marriage is vague and insufficient; since it does not declare

what shall constitute a valid widow marriage. The rite of matrimony is held sacred in all countries and by all nations. It is one of the ten *Sanscars* or sacramental rites of the Hindus. Its details are no where left to the option of individuals; yet such would be the case if the Bill for the removal of all legal obstacles to the marriage of Hindu Widows be passed into law as it now stands. The ceremony which at present prevails among Hindus, can not be performed in the case of a widow taking another husband. "The holy nuptial texts" says Menu in Chap. 8 Verse 226, "are applied solely to virgins and no where on earth to girls who have lost their virginity." Again in Chapter IX Verse 47. "Once is the partition of an inheritance made, once is a damsel given in marriage, and once does a man say 'I give.' These three are by good men done once for all and irrecoverably." It will, therefore, be necessary to prescribe a new ritual in opposition to the dictates of Hindu Law and Religion to prevent its being a source of much litigation, which it will otherwise necessarily lead to. Such a result cannot surely be the object of the Bill which is now before your Honorable Council. Your Petitioners also beg leave to submit that many Hindu widows who, if remarried at an early age under the proposed law, might regard their second union as a degradation and wrong, when at a mature age they come to know the religion and laws of their country.

8. Under these circumstances your Petitioners beg leave to submit that the "Bill to remove all legal obstacles to the marriage of Hindu widows" should not be passed into law, and that your Petitioners and the rest of their countrymen, who prefer to follow the established laws and usages of their country, will be permitted to continue in the enjoyment of their civil rights as they have heretofore done.

And your Petitioners, as in duty
bound, shall ever pray.

STRAY THOUGHTS,

ON

CHILD MARRIAGE

IN

BRITISH INDIA.

Job CHARNOCK was going up from Calcutta to a place now known as Barrackpore in a boat in the early days of the East India Company. At midstream the shrieks of a female reached his ears, and he ordered his boatmen to land the boat on the bank from where the wails came. He saw the corpse of a Hindoo on a funeral pyre in flames, and a young female child of thirteen being forcibly dragged by ruthless Hindoos towards the pyre for cremation with her deceased lord. The men were exhorting her to die a *suttee,* and obtain eternal fame for chastity, and exalt the glory of her deceased husband's and her father's family. The girl in utter despair, surrounded as she was by her executioners, was rending the air with her frantic cries and shrieks, and imploring Heaven to come to her rescue, free her from their grasp, and save her from being burnt alive. Job Charnock at this juncture appeared on the scene, took the girl into his boat, and rowed away to the country-seat of the Governor of Bengal. He educated her, and afterwards married her ; and she proved a loving and a faithful wife, and died in the beautiful country-seat, which after the name of Charnock, is to this day known by the Bengalees as *Chanuk,* and by the Hindoostani sepoys as *Achanuk.* The English know this place as Barrackpore, where our Viceroys at times retire for rest.

Similar atrocious murders of Hindoo widows were committed by their relatives with impunity in all parts of India under the cloak of religion until the year 1829, when Lord William Bentinck's Government passed a law making the act a crime and a felony, and aiders and abettors, felons, punishable, as principals, with death by the gallows. Lord William Bentinck was no coward son of Mars. His stern sense of duty as protector of the weak, the down trodden, and the helpless, living under the ægis of the British Nation, impelled him to action, and, viewing with disdain the prospect of a Hindoo rebellion which some of his chicken-hearted councillors whispered in his ears, he with a bold stroke of his pen rid the country of the inhuman rite The descendants of the Hindoos, who at the time cursed him in secret, now hold him up as the founder of the British reign in the hearts of the Hindoo race, and bless the nation that sent such a man to their country to govern with principles of righteousness and humanity.

At the present day, though such horrid deeds are no more heard of, there are nevertheless practices amongst the Hindoo subjects of the British Crown throughout the length and breadth of British India which are blots in the present British Administration of India. The British Nation has no idea of the extent of suffering to which innocent female children are subjected in the name of Hindoo religion, nor of the extent of loss of life attendant upon the observance of such Hindoo customs. The annual administration report of each province in British India gives the number of theft cases and each of the other offences complained against, in which perpetrators of crimes were detected or undetected, and in which punishment was brought home to the offender or otherwise, but no administration report of any province in British India gives us any idea of the number of Hindoo female children married in each year, nor of the age at which any particular number of them are married from the age of two to the age of fourteen. No system has yet been inaugurated for the registration of Hindoo marriages and there is no chance of knowing the number of Hindoo female children married in each year in India, nor the age at which any particular number of them are married. There is no chance of knowing how many Hindoo child wives of three years, how many of four years, and so on up to fourteen years become widows in every year in India. We cannot know of the number of child wives that die in the throes of child birth between the age of ten and fourteen. We do not think we can know of the number of infants of any particular race that die each year in British India within one month of their birth, within two months and so on up to the third year of the existence of such infants.

We fear, that if the Government of India be called upon to furnish information on these points it would plead its present inability to do so, and until the Government be directed by the Home Authorities to formulate measures to obtain accurate information on all these subjects it will take no steps to this end, so indifferent the Indian Government seems to be in these matters.

Our Government is under the impression that the high education it is giving to the people of this country will awaken in them a high sense of their responsibilities as fathers for their children's well-being, and that there will be no occasion for interfering with parental rights of the Hindoos over their children. Our Government has been acting on this impression. The continual flow of lectures by Hindoo young men from the year 1850 to the present date on public platforms against child marriage and enforced widowhood and the virtuous indignation the lecturers displayed on such occasions on the evils of Hindoo child marriage and the unanimous vote of censure which the audience on such occasions passed against such practices induce a belief in high officers of Government that the days of child marriage are doomed and that British India will in a short time be freed from the yoke of such inhuman customs and of streams of evils which flow from such a system.

At the risk of being long and tiresome I will reproduce here the proceedings of two meetings of educated Hindoos from the Indian Mirror of September and October of 1878, to shew the attitude of educated Hindoos in connection with the subject of child marriage.

[From the Indian Mirror, Thursday, the 26*th* September 1878.]

"Proceedings of a Meeting of the Students of Calcutta against child marriage."

"At the Instance of the Students' Association a public meeting of the Students of Calcutta was held at the Albert Hall on Saturday last at 6-30 P. M. The Hall was crowded to suffocation and hundreds had to go away from want of space to stand in."

"Dr. Mohendra Lal Sirkar was voted to the chair. The chairman opened the proceedings of the meeting with the remark that as one interested in the welfare of the country he considered child marriage a great source of evil and that he was impelled by a sense of duty to be present in the meeting. The movement he said was a right one and it originated in the most proper quarter."

"The Secretary then read a *precis* of the letters received from different schools and colleges in different parts of the country and it was seen from it that the movement was held with universal joy and unbounded enthusiasm. Meetings were held in different Schools and Colleges in the Mofussil and all were unanimous in adopting the line of procedure indicated by the Students' Association."

"Utmost enthusiasm prevailed during the three hours during which the meeting lasted and the following resolutions were then proposed and carried by acclamation. The Resolutions were all moved, seconded and supported in neat eloquent, and earnest speeches by students representing the different colleges of Calcutta and it is worthy of note that all of them were unmarried except the supporters of the first and second Resolution.

"Resolution 1."

"That this Meeting deeply impressed with the pernicious character of the custom of Child Marriage, convinced that it lies even in the humble power of students to take steps to check it, resolves to organise a movement amongst students to put down a custom so prejudicial to their best interests whether as students or as men."

"Proposed by Baboo Byomkesh Chakravarti, M. A., (Presidency College) seconded by Baboo Bidoo Bhoosun Mukherjee (Cathedral Mission College) and supported by Baboo Jogendro Nath Bose."

"Resolution 2."

"That this Meeting convinced of the importance and necessity of forming a band of young men pledged not to marry at too early an age with a view to help this movement and gradually to influence public opinion in its favor, resolves That the following form of pledge be adopted to be signed by such students as are in a position and feel themselves able to enter into this solemn obligation."

"Deeply impressed with the pernicious character of the custom of child marriage and with the evils that have followed in its train, convinced of the solemn duty I owe to myself and to my countrymen to discourage so far as may be in my humble power a custom so hurtful to students, so prejudicial to the best interests of my countrymen at large, I hereby solemnly declare that I shall not marry nor allow myself to be given in marriage till I have completed the age of twenty one years, my present age being———"

"Proposed by Baboo Narendrolal Dey (Presidency College) seconded by Dr. Tumizoddin (Medical College) and supported by Baboo Jogendra Chunder Bose B. A. (Presidency College)"

"Resolution 3."

"That the Members of the Committee of the Students' Association (*ex officio*) and the following gentlemen form themselves into a Permanent Standing Committee with power to add to their number for the purpose of taking such steps as may be deemed necessary to help and promote the movement that has been inaugurated and there be two secretaries to the Standing Committee, one of them being the secretary to the Students' Association for the time being, and the other to be appointed by the Standing Committee"

"Proposed by Baboo Nrityalal Mukerjee (Free Church Institution) seconded by Baboo Somendro Nath Tagore (St. Xaviers College) and supported by Baboo Bijoy Gobindo Bose. General Assembly's Institution.

"The following are the gentlemen in the commitee. A. M. Bose Esqr. M. A. Barister at Law, President, Students Association, Baboo Kally Churn Banerjee M. A. B. L. Vice-President Students' Association, Surendra Nath Banerjee B. A. Vice-President-Students, Association, Gooroo Dass Banerjee B, L, Vice-President Students' Association (now Honble justice Gooroo Dass Banerjee D. L. Vice-Chancellor Calcutta University) Byomkesh Chakravarty M. A., Suruth Chunder Chatterjee (Lucknow) Gooroo Prosunno Puttadar (Krishnaghur) Jogender Chunder Bose M. A., Tarakissore Chowdry, Kally Sunkur Sookool, Syamul Dhun Mittra, Nritya Lal Mukerjee, Somendro Nath Tagore. Monorunjun Dass (Secretary Bhowanipore Students' Association),"

"It must be noted here that an amendment to the second resolution was proposed by one Bepin Chunder Pal who wished to add the following words in the form of the Pledge, "and I will not marry nor allow myself to be given in marriage to a girl who has not completed her fourteenth year."

"The Resolution was subsequently withdrawn when the impracticability of the amendment was explained by diffrent speakers."

Baboo Rajnaran Bose of the Adi Brahmo Somaj and the Rev. Dr. K. M. Banerjee, who were present at the meeting spoke strongly in support of the amendment. The remarks which Baboo Rajnaran made in Bengali were very humorous and called forth roars of laughter. He exhorted the students to beware lest their zeal and enthusiasm evaporate like camphor. Dr. Banerjee exhorted them to have 'patience' He remarked that he was glad to notice a spirit of self-reliance growing up amongst the students of the present generation. In his younger days the students looked up to Government for suport in all sorts of reform."

"Babu Surendra Nath Banerjee in proposing a vote of thanks said that the most difficult part of the business yet remains to be done ; the difficulty was to carry on the movement with caution, earnestness and zeal." He exhorted the Students not to flinch nor to flag. As a Vice-President of the Students, Association he said, that that body did not arrogate to itself the functions of a Reformer but it has taken up the question of Child marriage into its hands because of all others this was the subject which affected the interests of students most seriously."

The Meeting broke up at 9 30 P. M. and twenty five of the young men present expressed their willingness to sign the pledge."

From the Indian Mirror, Tuesday the 15th and Thursday the 17th October 1878. From a correspondent

10 October 1878"

"BIRBHUM"

"On the requisition of the Calcutta Students' Association, a meeting of the gentlemen of Suri was convened by the pupils of the Birbhum Government School in September last, in the Birbhum Government School premises, for considering the subject of early marriage and the advisability of the students signing a pledge not to marry before the age of twenty-one. The meeting was largely attended by respectable Native gentlemen of the station, and presided over by Babu Kulodanund Mukerji, an Ex-Subjudge. After the delivery of addresses by some of the gentlemen present, it was resolved that the pupils should not sign the pledge without obtaining the consent of their parents and guardians. The following is the substance of the speech delivered by Babu Khetter Mohun Gangoly which produced a telling effect on the audience.

"Mr. President and Gentlemen.—We have been called here to-day to give expression to our views on the subject of early marriage amongst students of our schools. The subject has been one of great interest to me, and it is with no ordinary delight that I accept the invitation. I commend the spirit with which the matter has been taken up by the pupils of this School, and without any further observation I proceed to address them.

"The move now made by the Calcutta students' Association for the repression of early marriage, which has been one of the many causes to which the present degenerate state of the natives of this country is attributable, inspires me with the hope that there is looming in the distance, it may be, a more happy and prosperous era for the country. In days gone by, when the Aryans first settled in the Valleys of the Indus and the Ganges, and framed comprehensive rules for their conduct in life, early marriages were quite unknown. The Shastras, which the Rishis promulgated for the government of the people of India, went so far as to prohibit them. By the laws of Manu it was ruled that a man was first to finish his education, and then take to him a wife ; and the Hindus of old never thought of marriage for themselves or their children until they had attained the age of twenty-five, and when having completed their education, they were in a better position to judge for themselves, and strike out a course of life most advantageous to themselves and to their fellow-creatures. In those days women enjoyed greater privileges and liberty of action than now. The pages of the Mahabharat and the Ramayan tell us of the age at which men and women joined hands at the hymæneal altar and the different modes in which they did so.

" Females of the age of those who are in Europe considered marriageable could choose their husbands from among the male guests invited by their parents. The *Sayamvaras* of Domayanty and other renowned ladies will doubtless recall to your mind the numerous instances in which educated ladies of high rank exercised the privilege of choosing their partners in life. Your Head Master, Babu Sib Chunder Shome, has already quoted authorities to show that early marriage was never countenanced by your ancestors ; and that it is because early marriage was unknown amongst them that they came to be a great nation. Whence, then, has this baneful practice of early marriage sprung up—a practice which has taken such a deep and widespread root in our land ? This may at first sight appear to admit of no satisfactory answer. But when we recollect the changes which India has undergone from the time of the extinction of our independence : when we consider the misfortunes it laboured under during centuries of Mahomedan misrule, when we contemplate the struggles which the Hindus had to make to prevent any fusion of the races and the shifts they resorted to in order to attain that end, the difficulty vanishes, and we see at least two of the expedients they adopted. The Moslems, who then governed, were far from being a chivalrous nation. They often attempted the chastity of Hindu ladies, and the pages of history are replete with instances of Hindu ladies having perished by consigning themselves to fire rather than submit to dishonor at the hands of their lawless conquerors. It was in order the better to secure their ladies from harm that the Hindus of those days first introduced the zenana system and the practice of early marriage. Once wedded to these systems, the Hindus became staunch adherents to what had obtained the sanction of age. In course of their degeneracy during this dark age the great majority of them ceased to cultivate the language in which their ancestors had sung praises to God, and thus it was that the sacred texts were left in the hands of those who could retire from the scene and remain secure from intolerant enemies. The revolution, which followed the fall of the Hindu sovereignty compelled many a Hindu to take to the study of Persian, and thus eke out the means of subsistence or perhaps earn State honors. Sanskrit then became a dead language. The sacred texts were either destroyed, lost, or removed to places unknown. The Rishis were lost sight of even in the mountain fastnesses and impregnable forests. There remained, then, for the guidance of the Hindus, in matters moral and religious, but a few who had any pretension to a knowledge of the ancient Aryan lore. In course of time death snatched away one by one the few able Pundits that survived the downfall of the Hindu Empire; and their successors, under the consequent inauspicious circumstances that attended their endeavours at the mastery of the Sanskrit language, were certainly not the best guides to the fallen Hindu race in their affairs, temporal and spiritual. These men, possessed but a smattering knowledge of a few straggling works on Hindu Shastras, made their own compilations, annotations, and commentaries, and only too often, from inability to grasp the subject, rendered erroneous explanations, and in order to gain renown, engrafted on them opinions which, at the time were best calculated to suit the circumstances of the people among whom they lived. Rughunundun Bhuttacharji was a person of this class. He it was that preached the doctrine that when a man married a female child at the age of eight he obtained that reward in Heaven which Monoka and Dakhya attained by the gift of Gowri to Siva, and that when a man kept his daughter unmarried till the age of twelve he paved his own way and that of his ancestors to the seventh generation to Hell. Ignorant men, through fear of incurring the wrath of Heaven, disposed of their female progeny in marriage, not only before their twelfth, but even before their eighth year."

"Thus, early marriage having taken deep root in Hindu society, and having the colour of sanction of Hindu religion, gradually became a part of the social and religious institutions of the country."

"Unupurva marriage or betrothal of children even before their birth accompanied with religious ceremonies takes place even now in the 19th century among the Boidik Brahmins; and instances of baby-marriage among the higher castes in Bengal are not of infrequent occurrence. Even in this school there are married boys of the age of eight; and in this assembly are grown up men who were married at the age of ten. Bengali parents think that they have the right to marry their children to whomsoever and whenever they please. The good which parents alone can do to their children with that hearty care and solicitude which none other can bestow is marred in most cases by early marriage, when the education of the children is incomplete and when they are incapable of realizing the duties and responsibilities they have undertaken, or comprehending the injury, that their physical and intellectual nature are likely to suffer, and the pecuniary embarrassments that may arise. I do not however for one moment attribute any unworthy motive to parents in this I say through best of motives and mistaken notions of the fitness of things they hurry on the marriage of their chlidern. Early marriage was prevalent among the English, and to repress it the British nation had to pass a law holding null and void all marriages of infants under the age of twelve in the case of females, and fourteen in that of males. The French had to go further, and in the Code Napoleon it is laid down that any child married during his or her minority might, within six months after attaining the age of 25 at pleasure dissolve the marriage, if there be no children by the union. In India, however there is no such law We do not regret its absence when we see around us so many young boys, yet unsaddled with wives, striving head and heart to find out the effective means of curtailing the unbounded and arbitrary power of parents in this matter. The present occasion is, therefore, one of joy to every man who has bestowed a thought on the subject. Early marriage has the same effect on the married couple as the grafting process has on seedlings which grow into trees. Seedlings left to the fostering care of nature when arrived at maturity yield better and more durable fruit than grafts which are unnaturally forced, and consequently made to yield untimely fruits which erelong wither away. We see the same ill effects from early marriage. Boys in their teens become fathers, girls become mothers still earlier, both become old before they have tasted the real pleasures of youth. So far for the physical aspect of this all, important question. Our Civil Surgeon, Dr. G. C. Roy, who from the nature of his education and his professional experience is better able to afford information on this subject, has already given you his views. Now, let us see what effect it has upon our boys in respect to their morals. The association of married boys with the unmarried has often a very deleterious effect on the latter. The bachelors from idle curiosity question their wedded associates about the mysteries of married life, and learn from them things they should not dream of, and become possessed with longings which distract their attention from their studies and create artificial cravings. Boys, I beseech you to shun the company of married boys whom the dalliance of the Bashurghur, the flirtations of sisters-in-law, and the blandishments of wives have made effeminate and rendered unfit for the austere, the simple, the blessed life of a student. Shun them as you would shun your worst enemy, for they will poison your mind, and overcast the haven of your innocent thoughts with dark clouds, which will raise tempestuous storms and destroy your soul's peace. It is true we see instances of young boys who, notwithstanding these disturbing elements, have successfully passed their academical examinations. But these are of rare occurrence, and are the exceptions which prove the general rule that early marriage has a baneful effect on the prospect of many a young student, makes them mere abortions in the intellectual world, and sends them forth into cities and towns like famished wolve s in quest of service. This is a fact beyond dispute. The number of applications accompanied by recommendations, which an advertisement for a kerani on a miserable pittance of Rs. 15 or 20 attracts from various parts of the country, affords irrefutable proof of the deplorable influence of this great social evil."

"It may be said that a state of celibacy up to the 21st year of their age would lead students to habits of immorality. I scout the idea. The tendency to immorality, which must be the consequence of an unnatural and artificially created craving, is as much for the married student as for the unmarried when they are not taken care of by their parents and guardians, and are allowed to fall in bad company. But as students devoted to the noble cause of learning, as members of a sacred society united together by the bonds of a brotherhood keenly alive to the high sense of moral excellence—the very ideal of an ardent imagination, as votaries in the temple of science, whose duties should engage the whole man, body and soul, you will, I am fully assured, never so far degrade yourselves as to forget your position, nor fail to reprobate the conduct of such as stray from the right path. If there be any whom all these considerations will not restrain, on him my words are lost, and to such a person I do not address myself."

"The Students' Association at Calcutta have asked you to co-operate with them, and to sign a pledge not to marry before the age of twenty-one. I do not see how you, who are dependants on your parents even for your existence, can accede to this request without obtaining the assent of your parents. Your parents wishes on this point ought, therefore, to be first ascertained, and until this is done nothing can be said by any one of us who are present at this meeting. Your fathers will, I fear, set their face against such a proposal. Mothers in Bengal have, in matters domestic absolute authority ; and it is through the influence of mothers that boys are married during their infancy. The avarice for gold ornaments, gold and silver plates known as *Dan Samigri*, and cash as *Gon Pon* at the time of their son's marriage, presents at every occasion of festivity, and pecuniary assistance in times of need from the bride's father, and the desire of securing docile maids of all work free of cost, induce many mothers to contract early marriages for their sons. Such mothers seldom bestow a thought on the future of their offsprings, and it is idle to hope that under the influence of such, Bengali fathers will keep their sons unmarried till their twenty-first year, or consent to the signature of the pledge by their sons. I would therefore suggest to you the advisability of proposing to the Students' Association a Memorial for presentation to the Vice-Chancellor of the University with a prayer for the passing of a rule prohibiting the admission of married boys to the Entrance Examination, and another to the Director of Public Instruction for a rule to stop the admission of married boys, and continuance in Government and Aided Schools of such as may be married after the enforcement of the rule."

Now, let us see what lesson the proceedings of the Students' Association of Calcutta held in September 1878 teach us. It shewed :—

1stly. An earnest desire on the part of the Hindu students of all the schools and colleges throughout the province of Bengal to prevent their parents and guardians from marrying them before they had obtained their full physical growth, before they had finished their education, and before they had begun to earn the means of supporting themselves and their families.

2ndly. An earnest endeavour, with the advice and under the guidance of gentlemen of superior culture and worldly experience, and of the leaders of public opinion, to remain unsaddled with wives, and unencumbered with cares, anxieties, and pecuniary embarrassments consequent on the married state during their academical career.

3rdly. The promptitude with which the members of the learned professions, medicine, law and divinity, members of the British Indian Association, members of the Indian Association, members of the Brahmo Samajes, graduates of the University, and members of the Hindu community of Calcutta, responded to the call of the students of Bengal for help in their deliberations in connection with the course to be taken to prevent their marriage during their scholastic career.

4thly. The impracticability of finding unmarried Hindu girls in Bengal of the age of fourteen.

5thly. The uselessness of the endeavour of students and their distinguished supporters without the help of Goverment, but only with the aid of a pledge not to marry or allow themselves to be given in marriage before they have completed the age of twenty-one.

To the reader I leave the task of drawing the *morale* from the proceedings of the meeting of the students of Birbhoom held in September 1878.

More than twelve years have elapsed since these events took place; and the question of child marriage, in so far as it affects Hindu students, remains in the same state in which the students found it when they took it up. But where are the friends and well-wishers of Hindu students? Where are the Presidents, Vice-Presidents, and other office-bearers of the Students, Association who held their meeting in September 1878 at the Albert Hall? Have these gentlemen, whom the rising generation of Bengal look up to for the welfare of their Country, ceased to feel an interest in the student's cause! No, it cannot be; untoward events must have stared them in the face, and compelled them to keep back till an opportunity offers to enable them to prove themselves equal to the trust reposed in them by their young friends the Hindu Students of Bengal. I have heard people say these gentlemen finding the inutility of the Student's pledge, in their unwillingness to lose touch with the Hindu Community by invoking the aid of the Government in its educational department as suggested in the address to the students of Birbhum and seeing no hope of having the co-operation of fathers of Hindu students who never let slip an opportunity of making money in their bargains for the marriage of their sons during their academical career have washed their hands off the matter in utter despair. I do not think it has come to this, but if it be so, it is a matter of deep regret.

Let us now for a moment dismiss this subject from our mind's eye and turn to Miss Rukhmabai's tale of woe of the Hindu child wife in her letter to the National Review reproduced in the Indian Statesman of the 27th September 1890.

"Rukhmabai tells the following pitiful narrative of the lot of the Hindu child wife"

"In considering how child marriage affects the young wife we shall find, as might be expected, that the Hindu woman is even more degraded than the man. Indeed, no words can describe the mischief done by the system. It is the sole cause of the present deterioration of women in India. If child marriage is injurious to a man, it is ten thousand times more so to a woman. It has degraded her to such an extent that she has almost lost the dignity of humanity, and has come to be considered an inferior being. Indeed men regard her as much as they regard one of their domestic animals. The birth of a baby girl is always most unwelcome. The father gnashes his teeth and stamps his feet. The mother is sorely disappointed, and although her tenderness may bring its sure wealth of love, she curses both herself and the child. There is moreover a notion prevalent that women who bear only girls are sinful and this intensifies the grief. As the baby grows into a little girl the anxieties of the mother increase day by day.

"The girl as a rule, is married when she is eight years old. From what she has seen of life in her small experience she has a greater horror of going to her mother-in-law. The mere mention of her name is often enough to throw the child into a fever, and she tries every possible contrivance to delay her departure. She knows only too well the fate that awaits her. No play, no amusement, no kind words, no sweet smiles, not enough food, not even a quiet corner to rest in. Continually before her there will be the stern and angry face of the mother-in law, who will find nothing but fault with her, and punish her in the most cruel manner imaginable—from slapping to branding and starving or beating to death. At hand there will be young brothers and sisters-in-law on the alert to add to the wrath of their mother by telling fictitious tales of the child's misbehaviour towards them. She will be kept at hard work from morning till night and be rewarded by upbraiding and taunts. She will not be allowed to speak freely with any of the family or with any one else. Such will be her life No wonder that the, poor child dreads it. Nevertheless she has to face it. Her only consolation is to tell her mother about the treatment she receives in her husband's house. When the opportunity comes she pours out all her grievances with sobs and sighs in the hope of getting redress. But alas! there is none. The mother has no power to help her. The only consolation she can give is to say:- "It was no fault of mine or yours that you were born a woman. But since it has pleased God to send you as a woman into this world you must bear it as others have done. As time passes you may find your husband good and kind to you, and then you may feel amply rewarded for all these present sufferings," The poor girl, somewhat comforted by this kind advice, patiently awaits the brighter future pictured by her mother, whose sufferings have probably been similar. The time comes when the young people are united, and the promised happy time arrives. The young wife exerts herself to please her husband. If he loves her the promise is fairly fulfilled. She finds some comfort in his assurances of a happy future before them, when he may be able to earn a living for her, and when the mother-in-law can no longer disturb her happiness. But husbands who follow in the footsteps of their mothers are not rare. There are many faults which may be found by such a husband. His wife may not be handsome enough for him. She may not belong to a well to-do family, and may not have brought him a good dowry. She may not be clever nor obedient enough for him: and the faults grow in his sight as months go by, till he determines to put up with her no longer. She is cast aside and is superseded by another wife. Is there no one on earth who can help her? She has her parents. Will they not receive their own flesh and blood? She goes to them to seek refuge but public opinion is too strong, and though they love her dearly, they do not dare to relieve her, except with words of comfort. The mother's heart melts with grief and the father is in deep distress, but they can only say to their child, "Parents give birth, but do not shape destiny. Each individual brings his or her own destiny into the world. Whatever your misdoings in the former life have been, you must, my dear, suffer the penalty in this life. Try and bear it patiently and your future life will be a happy one. We have done our parental duty in giving you in marriage to the best person we could find; and after marriage there is no place on earth for a woman but her husband's house, and the only salvation for her is to live and die under his roof. Therefore, my child, be brave and face your misfortune without complaint."

"To live and die under the roof of her husband is the only

salvation for a woman! She has lived all these dreary years under her husband's roof; but she has not yet died there. As for living under it the thought is absolutely repugnant to her. Life has not the slightest attraction for her. Had she not better secure the "complete salvation" as soon as possible? The end is easy. She drowns her-self in the nearest well, tank or river, or takes a strong dose of opium. Thus is closed the brief chapter of sorrow and misery. Thank God, such is not the fate of every Hindoo woman. Let us turn to those who are still dragging along the weary path of life. This custom of child marriage causes many a Hindoo girl to become a mother at the age of fourteen, and she may bear a dozen or more undeveloped and sickly children, half of whom are born only to add to the misery of the poor creature, and to leave the world after having brought nothing but trouble and anxiety into it. It would be marvellous indeed if the young wife were not broken down by such ceaseless physical and mental strain. It has been shown that the education and mental culture of the boy-husband are hindered by premature marriage, and it can easily be inferred that the education and mental and moral development of the girl-wife become next to impossible. Thus any effort to educate the Hindoo woman before the abolition of child marriage seems like putting the cart before the horse."

"It remains for us to consider how child marriage, which has ruined the Hindoos, morally and physically, is to be got rid of. We must realise the fact that the race, by the long prevalence of this pernicious custom, has been weakened to such an extent that to rise up against that custom with united strength has become next to impossible. Owing to the spread of Western education, few individuals amongst the Hindoo community are ready to sacrifice themselves for this object. But after all they are a mere drop in the ocean. The majority of the people, being weak and ignorant, lack the moral courage to face the difficulties which stand in the way. The importance of moral courage, adherence to principles, and self-sacrifice for the good of their country, is not yet recognised by the masses. Still we are not justified in withholding the help we can give to bring about a better condition of things. Where is help to come from? I reply the British Government. True, it has undertaken not to interfere with religious beliefs of the natives of India. But child marriage is not sanctioned by the ancient Hindoo religion. It is mere custom. With custom the Government has to its credit more than once interfered in case of infanticide, homicide and suttee. These Hindoo practices were disastrous, but excepting the first they were self-imposed and not universal. The person sacrificing himself suffered premature death in this world hoping by that action to secure eternal rest. He or she died and the matter ended. But the Government considered itself bound to step in and prohibit those inhuman practices. Now the practice of child marriage is really far worse than the above mentioned abuses, for by that practice each and every individual is affected. It casts into the vital essence of young and old alike without distinction. How many a man has died heart broken and bankrupt through it. And what a number of women have to lead a life of utter misery and degradation! How many babes die before they are even conscious of their existence, simply as an inevitable result of this unnatural system. Considering all the evil this monstrous custom is doing to the nation, we may well ask whether it is right for the British Government to continue passive. There should be no delay in taking action. The measures adopted need not necessarily be harsh, but rather should be mild and persuasive. Without loss of time the Government might do a great deal in publicly showing disapproval of this custom of the

Hindoos" by declining to hold any marriage as binding until the ages of, say, eighteen in the boy, and fourteen in the girl. The small class of educated Hindoos are working with zeal to bring about this reform. They form associations, and pass resolutions. But an association is not a Government, and a resolution is not a law. The evil is too widespread and deep rooted to be got rid of by such means. I therefore earnestly appeal to the British Government to help us to put a stop to child marriage in India."

Thus has the poor girl of Southern India disburdened her troubled heart. The statement of her case combines moderation with admirable force. It is moderate in tone and style. Can we say it is untruthful? We cannot contradict her for she has told the truth and we join her in the appeal to Government for help. But the help we want is not of the kind which Miss Rukhmabai seeks. Several influential European officials of the British Indian Government seeing the present attitude of the Hindoos with respect to legislative interference in the matter of Hindoo child marriage, are counseling Government not to interfere for fear of creating a wide-spread disaffection among the Hindoo population against the Government. Under such circumstances we do not think there is any chance of any alteration being made in the law of marriage among the Hindoo people. Are we then without any hope of reform? Admitting the disinclination of Government to disaffect the Hindoos by legislative action with a view to reform the Hindoo marriage law, we do not think that after doing all that it has done for our intellectual elevation, it will remain indifferent and neglect to take such steps as without coming in conflict with Hindu religion and Hindu social usages will be effectual in arresting the progress of Hindu child marriage and causing the evils which are the necessary consequences of such a pernicious institution imperceptibly to disappear. It may be asked what is this mighty force which is capable of accomplishing such a marvellous feat.

The answer to this is simple. It is nothing but an alteration in the educational policy of the Government. It involves neither the curtailment nor the increase in the cost which the Government annually bears for the maintenance of its educational department. It is simply the direction to which the stream of education is to flow and this is a matter in which the Government has the supreme control and is one which our humane Government is bound to take up in right earnest as it will in the end remove the monstrous evil, the Hindu child marriage, from the face of India in no time.

We will now revert to the admirable and truthful letter of Miss Rukhmabai which we have reproduced in extenso. Miss Rukhmabai in this letter states that the child-wife's life ceases to be insupportable when her child husband finishes his education and becomes an earning member of the family. We see from this the necessity of taking steps to throw obstacles in the way of the marriage of Hindu boys before they have finished their School career. If this be done, many of the evils of Hindu child marriage will disappear and there will be no necessity for interfering by legislation with the rights of Hindu parents to marry their female children at any age they choose a right which they believe they are bound to exercise under the ordinance of their Hindu religion and social usage.

The only way to prevent the marriage of Hindu boys during their educational career is to induce the Government to alter its educational policy by closing the doors of its educational institutions against married students and to persuade the Universities to disaffiliate Schools and Colleges which admit married boys as pupils and allow pupils who marry to continue as students. In making this alteration in its educational policy the

Government will be acting in strict conformity to Hindu law ancient and modern which says a man must first finish his education and then take to him a wife.

Now the question arises who will ask the Government and the Universities to take up this step. I leave the question unanswered in the hope that some philanthrophist will take it up in right earnest for the good of his or her Hindu fellow creatures.

November 1-1890. KHETTER MOHUN GANGOLY

CALCUTTA.

FINIS.